ENDORSEMENTS

Jesus said, 'Seek first the kingdom of God and His righteousness, and all these things shall be added to you' (Matthew 6:33*)*. Michael's love for the Lord and His Kingdom is evident as he encourages God's people to steward well their God-given life and resources to accomplish their financial objectives and win friends for eternal life (Luke 16:9). This book is a remarkable contribution to that end.

Steve Nickel, Sr., J.D.
Gift Planning Counsel, Samaritan's Purse

What I love the most about Michael is that he is a real guy who really gets it. He has a way of making what many attorneys make complex easy to understand and interesting. I know because I used to be one. These two words "Estate Planning" have always bored me to tears. Michael breaks through that and offers something unique. It is a straightforward simple approach. He doesn't waste time on things we don't need to know. Most of all he helps us not just live a life, but leave a legacy.

Greg Lindsey, JD
Pastor of Discovery Church Colorado

Michael has written a very thorough, easy to understand, and Biblically-based book on the subject of estate planning. It is definitely a reference guide that I am going to keep and recommend to others.

Michael Occhipinti
Gift Planning Advisor
Wycliffe Bible Translators

In our interactions with Michael, it is apparent he is very knowledgeable and the utmost professional in the area of estate planning. His desire to glorify God through his work can be seen in his dedication and passion for what he does every day.

Joseph Padilla
VP of Development and Ministry Services
The Orchard Foundation

For what will it profit a man if he gains the whole world and forfeits his soul? (Matthew 16:26) More than two-thousand years ago, Jesus presented this soul-piercing question to humanity. For those who take this question seriously, Michael's concise and helpful book provides a real-life answer. While we certainly do not strive to store up treasure upon this Earth, the question becomes, if we have taken the Lord seriously in Matthew 16:26, how do we distribute our assets to the next generation in a way that glorifies the Lord? Whether your estate is large or small, or somewhere in between, you will find Michael's guide a helpful one in answering this question.

T. Ryan Lane, JD
T. Ryan Lane, P.C., Attorney at Law
Aztec, NM

With sweet irony, *Leaving a Lasting Legacy* is Michael Smith's own personal legacy for the rest of us, sharing his legal knowledge, his wisdom, and his heart for Kingdom service. As a life-long educator, I believe this wonderfully practical book will be of special interest to Christian colleges and universities as they reach out to their constituents for financial support. By helping potential donors see how they can provide for the Kingdom as well as for their families, Christian education will be richly blessed. Send this book out by the thousands! More importantly, this little volume is as motivating as it is practical. Even if you skim over the more technical bits until you need those precise details, the stewardship message flowing throughout the book will cause you to think more seriously than ever about what lasting legacy you will be leaving.

F. LaGard Smith
Professor of Law, Faulkner University's Jones School of Law
Author of over 30 books
Compiler and narrator of The Daily Bible

LEAVING A LASTING LEGACY

A Christian's Handbook
For
Gift And Estate Planning

Michael L. Smith, M.S., J.D.

Copyright © 2015 by Michael L. Smith
Published by Veritas Law Publishing
2950 Professional Place, Suite 207
Colorado Springs, CO 80904

Leaving A Lasting Legacy

Printed in the United States of America

ISBN-13: 978-1505349146

ISBN-10: 1505349141

All rights reserved. All rights reserved under International Copyright Law. May not be reproduced in any form without permission from the publisher.

Scripture quotations are from the ESV® Bible (The Holy Bible, English Standard Version®), copyright © 2001 by Crossway, a publishing ministry of Good News Publishers. All rights reserved.

This book, the stories herein, and the legal concepts herein, are provided for informational purposes only. Nothing contained in this book constitutes tax advice, legal advice, or a legal opinion on any subject matter or on any specific set of facts or circumstances. An attorney, accountant, and a financial advisor should be consulted regarding your particular situation.

To order copies of this book, visit amazon.com

Dedication

To my lovely wife Kari

You have been there through better and worse,
rich and poor...til death do us part.

To my sons Lookens, Kensley, Caleb, and Jake

I pray that I leave you guys a lasting legacy
that you will pass on to your kids someday.

Introduction

Perhaps for the first time in history, there is enough wealth amongst Evangelical Christians in the United States alone to fund the fulfillment of the Great Commission (Matthew 28:16-20). As we approach the end of the age, Christians have an unprecedented opportunity to change the world through their charitable giving.

The purpose of this book is twofold. First, it is meant to give the reader a basic understanding of the estate planning and gift planning process. Secondly, it is meant to inspire those with a Christian Worldview to look at their estate resources as a set of tools which can impact the world with the message of the Gospel.

The book is split into five chapters. Chapter 1, *A Lasting Inheritance*, introduces the concept of Biblical Estate Planning. Chapter 2, *Estate Planning Essentials*, gives the reader the nuts and bolts of the legal issues surrounding estate planning. Chapter 3, *Health Care Planning & Health Care Directives*, takes an in-depth look at the legal and practical issues during incapacity. Chapter 4, *Great Commission Estate & Gift Planning*, explores the impact of charitable giving at home and around the globe. Lastly, Chapter 5, *Leaving a Legacy*, encourages the reader to pass on their eternal values to the next generation.

Because I practice in Colorado, many of the examples and sample laws are taken from Colorado. However, these principles can be applied in any jurisdiction. Just make sure you consult with a Christian estate planning attorney in your state to ensure compliance with local laws. I hope this book challenges you to leave behind a wealth of generosity. Godspeed.

CONTENTS

CHAPTER 1
A Lasting Inheritance 1

The Preeminence of Christ 2
A Legacy of Stewardship 5
The Biblical Concept of the Tithe 6
The New Testament "Tithe" 8
The Generosity Gap 12
Great Commission Estate Planning 14

CHAPTER 2
Estate Planning Essentials 19

What Is Estate Planning? 19

Wills: An Overview 22
    What Is a Will? 22
    Who Can Make a Will? 23
    Who Needs a Will? 23
    Why Do I Need a Will? 24
    What Are the Benefits of Having a Will? 24
    Appointing a Personal Representative 25
    Choosing a Guardian 25

Wills FAQ 25
    What Happens If I Die Without a Will? 25
    What Is Probate? 26
    What Is a Probate Asset? 27
    What Is a Non-Probate Asset? 28
    Difference Between Probate and Non-Probate Assets 29
    Can I Just Re-Title All of My Assets into Joint
        Ownership? 30
    How Can I change My Will? 31
    When Should I Consider Creation of a New Will? 32
    How Can I revoke My Will? 32
    Should a Trust Be Created in My Will? 33

    Should I Mention Real Estate in My Will? 33
    Can I Make Specific Bequests (Gifts) in My Will 33
    What Is the Residuary or Remainder of My Estate? 34

Trusts: an Overview 34
    What is a Trust? 34
    Creation of a Trust 36
    Testamentary and Living Trusts 36
    Revocable "Living" Trust 37
    Transferring Assets into Revocable Trust 40
    Irrevocable Trust 41

Trusts FAQ 41
    What Are Some of the Different Types of Trust Tools? 41
        Credit Shelter Trust 41
        QTIP Trust 43
        Irrevocable Life Insurance Trust (ILIT) 44
        Charitable Remainder Trust (CRT) 47
        Charitable Lead Trust (CLT) 53
        Special Needs Trust 56
    Why Might I Need an ILIT? 61
    Can I Be the Trustee of My ILIT? 61
    How Does a Grantor Choose a Trustee? 62
    What Are Fiduciary Duties? 63
    Do I Need a Revocable Living Trust or a Will? 64

General Estate Planning FAQ 72
    Will My Family Have to Pay Estate Taxes? 72
    Techniques for Eliminating Death Taxes 75
        Gifting 76
        Credit Shelter Trust 76
        College Savings Plan 79
        Family Limited Liability Company 80
        Conservation Easements 81
    What Are Gift and Generation Skipping Taxes? 82
    What Do Clients Need to Do in Light of New Tax Laws 86
    How Can a Person Leave Property to Minor Children 88
    How Do I Choose a Trustee for My Children's Trust? 90

What Is a Spousal Elective Share?..90
Who Should Be the Beneficiary of My IRA?...................................91
What Is a Financial Power of Attorney? 92
Where Should I Keep My Estate Planning Documents?........92
Should I Have Funeral Instructions in My Will?........................93
Using an Attorney vs. Document Software?..............................93

CHAPTER 3
Health Care Planning and Health Care Directives 95

Health Care Planning 95
    The Andersons...95
    The Biblical Mandate to Care for Our Family 97
    Jesus' Command to Take Care of Family 100

Health Care Directives 101
    The Jacobs 101
    End of Life Planning..103
    Which Document Is Best for Me? 104
    Modern Day Miracles 105
    The Will to Live 107

CHAPTER 4
Great Commission Estate and Gift Planning.........................109

Go Change the World..110

Great Commission Estate Planning in Action 111
    Samaritan's Purse 112
    Young Life...114
    Wycliffe Bible Translators 117
    Carson-Newman University 119
    Liberty University...120

Estate Planning Generosity Gap 122

Ways to Give to Church or Ministry..123
    Gifts During Lifetime 123

Gifts upon Your Death 131
Generosity in Action 133
    How Much Is Enough? 133
    How Much Should I Give? 134
    The Generosity Matrix 135
    Radical Generosity Stories 136

CHAPTER 5
Leaving a Legacy 141

A Tale of Two Legacies 141
Communicate Your Legacy 145
Legacy Will 146
Family Meeting 149
Last Words 150

About the Author 155

Appendix A: Estate Planning Terms 157

Appendix B: Intestate Succession in Colorado 162

Appendix C: Credit Shelter Trust Flow Chart 163-164

Appendix D: Charitable Remainder Trust with Wealth
                Replacement Life Insurance Trust 165

Appendix E: Charitable Lead Trust 166

Appendix F: Federal Estate Tax Chart: 2013-2016 167

Appendix G: Spousal Elective Share 168

Appendix H: Donor Advised Funds vs.
                Private Foundations 169

Appendix I: Federal Income Tax Deductions
                for Charitable Gifts 170

Sources 171

CHAPTER 1

A LASTING INHERITANCE

Our days are numbered. One of the primary goals in our lives should be to prepare for our last day. The legacy we leave is not just in our possessions, but in the quality of our lives. What preparations should we be making now? The greatest waste in all of our earth, which cannot be recycled or reclaimed, is our waste of the time that God has given us each day.
Billy Graham

There is not a square inch in the whole domain of our human existence over which Christ, who is Sovereign over all, does not cry: Mine!
Abraham Kuyper

Live a legacy to leave a legacy.
Chad Sparks, Senior Pastor
Providence Church, Knoxville, TN

Nobody would remember the Good Samaritan if he'd only had good intentions; he had money as well.
Margaret Thatcher

Blessed be the God and Father of our Lord Jesus Christ, who has blessed us in Christ with every spiritual blessing in the heavenly places, even as he chose us in him before the foundation of the world, that we should be holy and blameless before him. In love he predestined us for adoption as sons through Jesus Christ, according to the purpose of his will, to the praise of his glorious grace, with which he has blessed us in the Beloved. In him we have redemption through his blood, the forgiveness of our trespasses, according to the riches of his grace, which he lavished upon us, in all wisdom and insight making known to us the mystery of his will, according to his purpose, which he set forth in Christ as a plan for the fullness of time, to unite all things in him, things in heaven and things on earth. In him we have obtained an inheritance, having been predestined according to the purpose of him who works all things according to the counsel of his will, so that we who were the first to hope in Christ might be to the praise of his glory. In him you also, when you heard the word of truth, the gospel of your salvation, and believed in him, were sealed with the promised Holy Spirit, who is the guarantee of our inheritance until we acquire possession of it, to the praise of his glory.

Ephesians 1:3-14

The love of money is the root of all kinds of evil.

1 Timothy 6:10

The Preeminence of Christ

Proverbs 13:22 reminds us that, "A good man leaves an inheritance to his children's children." In legal terms, an inheritance is a transmission of property to an heir upon a person's death. Leaving an inheritance to a loved one certainly encompasses the passing of physical property, but from a spiritual perspective, leaving an inheritance also has eternal implications. As Christians in America, most of us associate the word inheritance with money, real estate, cars, and other types of property that are transferred to the next generation when a family member dies. In God's economy, an inheritance encompasses our adoption into his family accomplished through the purchase price of His Son's blood. The purpose of this book is to briefly explore the connection between a physical and spiritual inheritance so that we are better equipped to leave a lasting legacy to both our children and our children's children.

When we broach the topic of estate planning, it is instinctive to immediately begin thinking about the distribution of physical property. However, the best starting point for end of life planning is the recognition that Christ is sovereign over all things, including our money, possessions, property, our children, and certainly our eternal security. Only when we include Christ as the cornerstone of our plan can move forward in confidence that we are approaching our estate planning with a heart for God's Kingdom and His people.

Adding a Christian preamble to a Last Will & Testament or Revocable Living Trust is a great way to establish Christ's preeminence regarding our final earthly wishes. A Christian preamble is simply a written statement of your Christian faith that is included in your Last Will & Testament or Trust document. In our materialistic society we have grown so preoccupied with the distribution of our material possessions that we have often forgotten that the only true and lasting wealth we can pass to the next generation is our testimony that Jesus Christ saves sinners and offers them abundant and eternal life by His grace. In the opening paragraph of your life's most important legal document, a preamble is your last earthly opportunity to put Christ first and to proclaim your faith to your friends and family. This can be a great source of comfort to a mourning family and powerful reminder of God's promise of eternal life.

A Christian Preamble is personal in nature and each person can write their own according to their wishes, however, below are a few examples of preambles that can be used as is or modified accordingly.

> I do hereby testify that I am a Christian. I have placed all my hope of life hereafter in Jesus Christ, the Son of God. His death and resurrection have given my life meaning and make my death a peaceful passage to eternal life in heaven. I want my family and friends to know that for me to live was Christ, and to die is gain.
>
> I want all who read this to know that Jesus Christ is my Savior. I have no doubt about my being saved by him or my being in heaven. I ask my children, whom I love, never to forget the

instructions Christ has given to us, "Go into all the world and preach the gospel to every nation." Share God's Word with everyone at home and abroad. May God grant you peace, love, and strength as he guides you through this life. Then at the end of time, we will be reunited in heaven.

I commit myself to God's care, secure in his love for me and trusting in the salvation purchased for me through Christ's suffering and death. I leave those who survive me the comfort of knowing that I have died in this faith and have now joined my Lord in eternal glory. I commend my loved ones to the protecting arms of God, knowing that he will continue to provide for them despite my absence; and I encourage them to place their faith and trust in him alone.

Realizing the uncertainty of this life, and with full confidence and trust in my Lord and Savior, Jesus Christ, in His death on the cross and shed blood as an atonement for my sins, and knowing that by faith I have eternal life through His sacrifice on the cross for me, do hereby make public and declare this to be my Last Will and Testament.

My heartfelt desire is that each of my loved ones might know the love of Jesus Christ and trust in His amazing grace. In His name only can any of us know the perfect assurance and the unspeakable joy which have become my inheritance. It is my hope and my prayer that Christ's love, which is most precious in my life, will be the most cherished legacy of all my loved ones. I thank the heavenly Father for His bountiful blessings.

I leave to all of my loved ones the words of our Savior, found in John 3:16. For God so loved the *world, that He gave His only begotten Son, that whoever believes in Him shall not perish but have eternal life. I leave those who survive me the comfort of knowing that I have died in this faith and now have joined my Lord in eternal glory.*

Regarding Christ, the Apostle Paul reminds us in Colossians 1:18, "He is the beginning, the firstborn from the dead, that in everything he might be preeminent." Jesus Christ is preeminent over everything, which includes our end of life planning.

A Legacy of Stewardship

A Christian Estate Plan is about much more than passing your worldly possessions to your surviving family. It's about leaving a lasting legacy both materially and spiritually, that will make an impact in eternity. With the proper perspective, your estate plan can both provide for your family and make an impact for the Gospel. For Christians, estate planning is the final act of stewardship over the resources that our Heavenly Father has entrusted to us.

The Psalmist reminds us, "the earth is the Lord's and the fullness thereof" and that God owns "the cattle on a thousand hills." Everything is His. Everything. We are simply stewards of his blessings during our brief lives. A steward is someone who manages the property or finances of another. By contrast, a King is a sovereign authority who reigns over people and property. When it comes to handling financial affairs and estate matters, many Christians make their plans as if they were in the position of King. However, when Christ is placed in His rightful position of preeminence as the King of Kings, we realize that our role is to make financial and estate planning decisions as a steward faithfully managing His property. Therefore, if you looked at your house as His house and your bank account as His bank account, how would that change how your property would be distributed upon your death?

As stewards, we must also remember that a good man leaves an inheritance to his children's children and those who do not take care of their families are worse than unbelievers. Therefore, upon our death, God does not expect us to give all of our estate back to Him. We are also called to take care of our family members, financially and otherwise. This is no different than what He expects of us during our lifetime.

The Biblical Concept of the Tithe

The biblical concept of giving God a tithe (which means "tenth" in Hebrew) from our income, helps give us a framework for striking the proper balance between giving back to God what is already rightfully His and taking care of the financial needs of our family. The tithe was first mentioned in Genesis 14 when Abram gave Melchizedek, the King of Salem, a tenth of his spoils from war. Additionally, in the Old Testament, the Israelites were required under the law to give a tenth of all that they produced.

> *Every tithe of the land, whether of the seed of the land or of the fruit of the trees, is the LORD's; it is holy to the LORD.*
>
> Leviticus 27:30

> *To the Levites I have given every tithe in Israel for an inheritance, in return for their service that they do, their service in the tent of meeting.*
>
> Numbers 18:21

> *You shall tithe all the yield of your seed that comes from the field year by year.*
>
> Deuteronomy 14:22

> *As soon as the command was spread abroad, the people of Israel gave in abundance the first fruits of grain, wine, oil, honey, and of all the produce of the*

> *field. And they brought in abundantly the tithe of everything.*
>
> 2 Chronicles 31:5

> *Bring the full tithe into the storehouse, that there may be food in my house. And thereby put me to the test, says the LORD of hosts, if I will not open the windows of heaven for you and pour down for you a blessing until there is no more need.*
>
> Malachi 3:10

In the Old Testament, eleven of the twelve tribes of Israel were given land as an inheritance. They were called to work the land and produce a bountiful harvest. The Levites, however, were called to serve in the ministry of the Lord and they did not receive any land. In other words, they were not called to the traditional work and labor that over 90% of the Israelites were called to. Their means of income and their inheritance were found in the tithe, which came from the harvest of the other eleven tribes. There were other tithes and offerings in the Old Testament as well, including tithes that were to be spent celebrating God's faithfulness with family, friends, and the fatherless and widows (Deuteronomy 14).

In the book of Malachi, God challenged the Israelites to put Him to the test by bringing the full tithe into the storehouse. The Israelites were robbing God by keeping back some of the tithe for themselves. But God reminded them that the full tithe is what He required. Not only that, he promised them abundant blessings if they did so. Now, I am not advocating for a health, wealth, and prosperity mindset to the tithe. For Jesus reminded us that in this life we will have many troubles. Financial riches are not a byproduct of the Christian life. But God did promise the Israelites and he does promise us, that he will take care of our needs if we trust Him with our financial future.

The New Testament "Tithe"

Tithing is not a very popular topic in American churches today. Anytime I have been in church when the pastor begins a sermon or a series on giving, there is a collective tension in the building. It just makes most of us down right uncomfortable to even discuss it. There is also a popular viewpoint in the church today that the tithe was an Old Testament concept that Christians are not obligated to continue under the New Covenant. I believe it is true that the New Testament does not have a "thou shalt tithe" text, however, to claim that the principles of the tithe are not found and even encouraged in the New Testament is simply not true to scripture.

Although the New Testament does not subscribe to a legalistic system of tithing, the concept of generous giving generally and the tithe specifically, is unequivocally reaffirmed in the New Testament. Similar to God's command to tithe to the Levites in the Old Testament, the Apostle Paul directs the church in Corinth to give to the saints (those who are ministers of the Gospel) out of their income.

> *Now concerning the collection of the saints: as I directed the churches of Galatia, so you also are to do. On the first day of the every week, each of you is to put something aside and store it up, as he may prosper, so that there will be no collecting when I come.*
>
> 1 Corinthians 16:1-2

Paul is directing the people of the church who make their living in the marketplace (which is most of them) to financially support the work of those who God has called to share his Gospel on a full time basis (i.e., church leadership, ministers of the Gospel, missionaries). Therefore, it seems clear that just like in the Old Testament, God wants his followers who have the ability to produce income (which is most of us) to provide for the financial needs of those who He calls to full time ministry (pastors, ministries, missionaries, parachurch organizations), through our tithes.

In 2 Corinthians 8, Paul encourages believers everywhere to give generously, even radically. The churches of Macedonia, despite their extreme poverty, "overflowed with a wealth of generosity." Though poor, they gave beyond their means to the work of the Gospel. Regarding their generous giving Paul urged the church in Corinth to do the same.

> *But as you excel in everything—in faith, in speech, in knowledge, in all earnestness, and in our love for you—see that you excel in this act of grace also. I say this not as a command, but to prove by the earnestness of others that your love also is genuine. For you know the grace of our Lord Jesus Christ, that though he was rich, yet for your sake he became poor, so that you by his poverty might become rich.*
>
> 2 Corinthians 8:7-9

In the next chapter, Paul clarifies what Christian generosity should look like.

> *The point is this: whoever sows sparingly will also reap sparingly, and whoever sows bountifully will also reap bountifully.* **Each one must give as he has decided in his heart, not reluctantly or under compulsion, for God loves a cheerful giver.** *And God is able to make all grace abound to you, so that having all sufficiency in all things at all times, you may abound in every good work. As it is written, "He has distributed freely, he has given to the poor; his righteousness endures forever." He who supplies seed to the sower and bread for food will supply and multiply your seed for sowing and increase the harvest of your righteousness. You will be enriched in every way to be generous in every*

> *way, which through us will produce thanksgiving to God. For the ministry of this service is not only supplying the needs of the saints but is also overflowing in many thanksgivings to God. By their approval of this service, they will glorify God because of your submission that comes from your confession of the gospel of Christ, and the generosity of your contribution for them and for all others, while they long for you and pray for you, because of the surpassing grace of God upon you. Thanks be to God for his inexpressible gift!*
>
> 2 Corinthians 9:6-15

Jesus also mentioned the practice of tithing while rebuking the Pharisees for tithing with the wrong heart.

> *But woe to you Pharisees! For you tithe mint and rue and every herb, and neglect justice and the love of God. These you ought to have done, without neglecting the others.*
>
> Luke 11:42

Jesus examines the Pharisees heart for tithing and finds that their giving lacks the love of God. They are simply giving out of ritualistic obligation. He prioritizes justice and the love of God above the tithe in the Christian life, but he does not condemn the practice of the tithe. In fact, he affirms it, when the giver's motives are pure.

It is also interesting to note that Jesus spoke about money more than any other topic during his earthly ministry. Let that sink in for a second. More than heaven, hell, marriage, sex, relationships, discipleship, the church, etc. You see, Jesus knew that how we handle our finances is evidence of where we ultimately put our faith and trust. Our generosity, or lack thereof, shows where our allegiance lies- either with the treasures of this world, or the treasures of His coming Kingdom.

> *Do not lay up for yourselves treasures on earth, where moth and rust destroy and where thieves break in and steal, but lay up for yourselves treasures in heaven, where neither moth nor rust destroys and where thieves do not break in and steal. For where your treasure is, there your heart will be also.*
>
> Matthew 6: 19-21

I believe that much of our modern view of tithing probably has to do with asking the wrong question. Instead of saying, 'How little can I give out of my income and still be in favor with God?', we should be asking 'God, how can I give generously to further your Kingdom and make your name known in the world?'. Again, I am not suggesting that the New Testament scriptures leave us with a tithing formula, but what I am saying is that the concept of Old Testament tithe was affirmed by Jesus, and that Paul encourages us to give generously from the blessings God bestows upon us to further God's work in the world.

It would seem that instead of the tithe being the end goal, God is calling us to give above and beyond that. To overflow with a wealth of generosity like the churches in Macedonia. Not out of legalistic compulsion, but out of love for Him and His people. The Israelites had this tithing thing down, much better than the Christian church today. But over and over again they failed to follow God.

Tithing for the sake of tithing does not get us on God's good list. What God wants is for His followers to love Him with a pure heart and in turn love others. It is a matter of having a generous heart and using our resources to point the world towards God's radical gift of grace.

The Generosity Gap

Many in the Christian church believe that the 10% figure from the Old Testament should be our starting point for giving and that we should strive to be generous in giving to God's Kingdom above and beyond the 10% baseline. Despite this widely held belief, there is a generosity gap between our resources and our giving. In other words, we as American Christians have been blessed beyond belief, yet we hold to our money with clinched fists.

Consider the following recent statistics on Christian giving:

- Only 5% of Americans tithe 10% or more of their income.
- Only 12% of born again Christians tithe 10% or more of their income.
- According to the State of the Plate annual church giving research: of those Christians who do tithe 10% of their income during life, only 25% tithe to church or ministry through their estate plan.
- The average weekly donation by Christians to their church is $17.
- Post 2008, 16% of Protestants have decreased their donations to non-profit organizations.
- Post 2008, 33% of Protestants have decreased their giving to churches.
- 11% of Americans have completely dropped all giving to churches.
- On average, Christians gave 3.3% of their income to their church during the Great Depression.
- Today, on average, Christians give 2.6% of their income to church, despite our unprecedented historic prosperity (even in the midst of recession).
- Half of the richest people in the world live in America.
- The average family income in America is about $51,000.
- If your family income is above $50,000 then you are in the top 1% of richest people in the world.

- The median family income in the world is about $1,200 per year.
- According to the World Bank, 1.2 billion people in the world live on less than $1.25 per day, while 2.4 billion people live on less than $2 per day.
- 80% of the world's evangelical wealth is in North America. In fact, according to Ron Blue, **if American evangelicals tithed, there would be enough funds to fulfill the Great Commission.**

I have also noticed that very few of my Christian clients desire to tithe a portion of their estate in their Last Will & Testament or Revocable Living Trust. Some believe that they have already tithed from their income during their lifetime, therefore, tithing from their estate is not necessary. True, a tithe from your estate is not necessarily required. However, giving a portion of your estate to God sets a precedent of generosity and thanksgiving for those you leave behind. Remember, Estate Planning is about leaving your stuff to your family, but Christian Estate Planning is about leaving a lasting legacy for your family. I am sure all Christians want their children to fear God and lead lives of generosity. Tithing from your estate is your last earthly chance to model that behavior for your children and encourage them to live their lives in allegiance to Christ's mission.

I am reminded of a story I heard from the pastor of the church I attended in my youth. An older man in our church was losing his battle to cancer with his family and loved ones gathered around his hospital bed. In his parting words the man said to them, "I have shown you how to live, now I must show you how to die." In other words, you have seen me model a life lived trusting in Jesus Christ, now I need to show you what it looks like to die trusting Him as well. I will never forget that story. What a beautiful picture of a man leaving a lasting legacy to his wife and children. A man focused on teaching his family to trust in their Savior even to his last breath. That is the goal of estate planning from a Christian perspective; to take care of our family and leave them with a legacy of generosity and faithfulness to God.

> **PLANNING POINT**
>
> Regarding Christian Estate Planning, it seems to me that there is a balance between taking care of our family and tithing from our increase to impact God's Kingdom. Both concepts are biblical. Therefore, many of my clients who plan from this perspective find it best to leave everything to their surviving spouse and provide in their estate planning documents that upon the surviving spouse's death a certain percentage of the combined estate goes to church and charity. For example, a husband and wife would leave their entire estate to each other. If husband dies first, wife would receive everything. Then upon wife's death, 10% of the estate would go to their local church and/or to various Christian ministries, and 90% to the children equally.

Great Commission Estate Planning

Once you have decided to tithe from your estate, the next step is to figure out how much. In my opinion, tithing 10% to your local church body and other Christian ministries and missionaries should be the baseline for giving, while leaving room for God to lead you to give above and beyond that amount. In his last moments on earth, our Lord Jesus explained to his followers:

> *...you will be my witnesses in Jerusalem and in all Judea and Samaria, and to the end of the earth.*
>
> Acts 1:8

I think this is a perfect example of how our parting words should make an impact for the Gospel. A believer's witness for

Christ starts with their own community (Jerusalem) and then like a pebble dropped into a lake, makes a ripple effect in the world around us. Giving first to our local church, then to ministries that impact our region (Judea and Samaria), then to mission efforts in other countries, is one way that we can be Christ's witnesses in accordance with Acts 1:8.

Just imagine the legacy you could leave behind if you approached the creation of your estate plan not just as a morbid exercise of leaving your stuff behind, but as your final mission to impact the world. Think about this for a moment. 2.4 billion people in the world live off of $2 per day without access to basic necessities. A gift in your estate plan to your church missions ministry or a mission's organization can change people's lives both practically and spiritually, forever. Your gift could allow a mission's organization to provide for the physical needs of a family that has never heard the name of Jesus and change the spiritual heritage of that family for generations to come.

> *But whoever has the world's goods, and beholds his brother in need and closes his heart against him, how does the love of God abide in him.*
> 1 John 3:17

Christ has called us to be his witnesses locally, regionally, nationally, and globally. Certainly this is our calling in life, and upon our death we can direct that our resources be used to continue to fulfill that purpose. In a scene from the movie Gladiator, the hero, Maximus Decimus Meridius, exclaims to a crowd of Romans, "What we do in life echoes in eternity." I believe that our death can also echo in eternity, if we are willing to view our estates with a Kingdom perspective.

So, how much should you give? I will address that in more detail in the following chapters. Ultimately it is a personal decision for you and your family, but giving should always be done with a heart of love for God and His people.

> *Each one must give as he has decided in his heart, not reluctantly or under compulsion, for God loves a cheerful giver.*
>
> 2 Corinthians 9:7

Our Father is concerned with our heart and motivation for giving, not a dollar amount. We should desire to give abundantly and sacrificially because He has poured out his blessing on our lives abundantly and sacrificially through His amazing grace in Christ Jesus.

John Wesley's Tithe

John Wesley was one of the greatest evangelists who has ever lived. At the age of 28, he decided that he could live on 28 pounds per day, which was a reasonable salary for an Englishman in his day. He made 30 pounds that year and gave 2 pounds away to the poor. The next year he made 60 pounds and gave 32 pounds to the poor. The next year he made 90 pounds and gave 62 pounds away to the poor. One year Wesley made 1,400 pounds, lived on 28 pounds, and gave away the rest.

He was once investigated by the English Tax Commissioners who thought that a man with his income should have plenty of silver dishes that he was not paying taxes on (silver was taxable). Wesley wrote them a letter stating, "I have two silver spoons….and I shall not buy more while so many round me want bread."

When he died at the age of 87, the only assets mentioned is Wesley's Last Will and Testament were the coins in his pockets and the ones in his dresser drawer. He had given away nearly 30,000 pounds during his life. In his will he wrote, "I cannot help leaving my books behind me whenever God calls me hence; but in every respect, my own hands will be my executors." At the end of his life, Wesley had very little money, but he passed on a spiritual legacy that endures to this day.

An Eternal Inheritance From Our Father

Did you know that the Bible mentions a Last Will & Testament? The writer of Hebrews uses a will as an illustration for God ushering in the New Covenant through Christ's death.

> *Therefore he is the mediator of a new covenant, so that those who are called may receive the promised eternal inheritance, since a death has occurred that redeems them from the transgressions committed under the first covenant. For where a will is involved, the death of the one who made it must be established. For a will takes effect only at death, since it is not in force as long as the one who made it is alive.*
>
> Hebrews 9:15-17

Through the "riches of his grace, which he lavished upon us," the Father gave us his Son, so that we "may receive the promised eternal inheritance." Following our Father's example, as his children, our estate plans should leave the next generation with the message of this eternal inheritance through faith in Christ. That is the legacy that the Father leaves to his children and it is the legacy that we must leave as well.

Bridging the Generosity Gap

There is a generosity gap in the American church today. I believe that planned giving, particularly through Christian estate and gift planning, can help bridge the gap and pave the way for the Gospel to be preached throughout the world. When "God calls us hence," what will be our legacy?

CHAPTER 2

ESTATE PLANNING ESSENTIALS

A good man leaves an inheritance for his children's children.
Proverbs 13:22a NIV

Go to the ant, O sluggard; consider her ways, and be wise.
Proverbs 6:6

If you fail to plan, you are planning to fail!
Benjamin Franklin

If riches increase, do not set your heart upon them.
Psalm 62:10b

It's OK to have wealth. But keep it in your hands, not in your heart.
S. Truett Cathy
Founder, Chick-fil-A Restaurants

Come now, you who say, "Today or tomorrow we will go into such and such a town and spend a year there and trade and make a profit"—yet you do not know what tomorrow will bring. What is your life? For you are a mist that appears for a little time and then vanishes. Instead you ought to say, "If the Lord wills, we will live and do this or that."
James 4:13-15

What is Estate Planning?

Estate planning is the process of preparing during your life for the distribution of your worldly possessions upon your death. Your estate includes all of the property that you own at the time of your death including real estate, bank accounts, investment accounts, business interests, life insurance policies, and personal property. Creating an estate plan for the eventual transfer of your assets to your family and loved ones is essential no matter what stage of life you are in, considering that your life here on earth is but a vapor.

A carefully crafted estate plan will allow you to bestow a legacy to your family and will provide direction about what happens to your assets in the event of disability, incapacity, or death. It can also provide you with the peace of mind that your intentions will be followed and that your family will be well taken care of in your absence. For Christians, an estate plan can also be a great tool for charitable planning.

An estate plan often includes the creation of some or all of the following documents:

Last Will and Testament - A document that defines how you want to distribute your estate, selects guardians for children, minimizes estate taxes, and establishes your personal representative.

Revocable Living Trust - A trust, created in your lifetime, which you may revoke or amend at any time. The use of a properly funded Revocable Living Trust allows your estate to bypass the probate process upon your death.

Durable Power of Attorney (Financial) - A document that grants someone you trust with the authority to make financial decisions on your behalf, even after you become incapacitated.

Medical Power of Attorney - A document which names someone to make health care decisions for you (your "health care agent") if you develop a condition that makes it impossible for you to speak for yourself. A Medical Power of Attorney is often combined with a Living Will (not to be confused with a Last Will and Testament), which describes your wishes regarding nutrition, hydration, artificial breathing, etc., if you are in a terminal condition or a persistent vegetative state.

The Importance of Proactive Planning

All adults (18 or older) should have an estate plan, even if it is only a basic Last Will and Testament. One of the most important things a person can do is provide clear direction to guide his or her loved ones in the event of illness, incapacity, or death. After all, an estate plan is not really for you, it's for the ones you leave behind. Creating an estate plan is a selfless act of love that will lessen your loved ones' burdens during one of the most challenging times of their lives. Additionally, most people find that peace of mind and satisfaction result from putting their affairs in order.

It is often said that everyone has an estate plan, because when a person dies intestate (without a will) the courts are required to follow mandatory statutory guidelines to determine the disposition of the deceased person's estate. Which means that predetermined guidelines would be followed to distribute your property, regardless of your wishes. Do you want ridged state laws to determine who will inherit your assets when you pass away? Do you want a judge to decide who your children will live with? Do you want the courts to appoint someone to make medical or financial decisions for you in a situation where you cannot make them for yourself? Do you want to leave your church or charity out of your plan? If you answered no to any of those questions, it's probably time to create your estate plan. An estate plan gives you the freedom to make these critical decisions and prepares you and your family for the future. Deciding to proactively create an estate plan allows you and not the court to make these all important decisions, and it will give you confidence that your affairs will be properly administered according to your desires. Furthermore, having an estate plan accomplishes several important goals, including:

- Written Documentation of Your Wishes
- Prevents Family Disputes
- Establishes A Neutral Administrator To Settle The Estate
- Provides For the Needs of Loved Ones
- Establishes a Guardian for Minor Children
- Reduces Delay in the Distribution of Your Estate
- Reduces Estate Administration Costs
- Vehicle for Charitable Giving
- Provides Peace of Mind That Your Estate Affairs Are In Order
- Estate Tax Savings (for Larger Estates)

The Planning Process

The creation of your estate plan typically begins with a consultation with an Estate Planning Attorney. Often times, the law office will have you complete a questionnaire before the initial meeting. During the initial meeting, the attorney asks several questions in order to learn about you, your family, and your financial situation. Once your goals and objectives are fully understood, the attorney will work with you and your other trusted advisors (i.e, financial planner, accountant, ministry planned giving coordinator, etc.) to develop an estate plan that protects, preserves, and passes on all that you have worked so hard for. Estate planning always works best as team sport, where your advisors are working together to achieve the results that you desire. Once a plan is set in to motion, it usually takes the attorney a few weeks to prepare all of the necessary documents for your signature.

WILLS -An Overview

Will - A document that directs how property shall be distributed upon a deceased person's death.

A Will is the foundational document for most estate plans. It is a legal instrument specifying how a person's property and assets should be handled after death. A testator (the person making the will) can give instructions on how the property should be divided, who should receive what portions or specific items, and even who will take care of any surviving minor children. A will can also establish a trust or make gifts to charity.

As discussed above, without a will, the state determines how property will be distributed. A carefully drafted will eases the transition for survivors by transferring property efficiently while avoiding many financial and administrative burdens. Despite these advantages, many estimates figure that at least seventy percent (70%) of Americans do not have valid wills.

Wills vary from extremely simple single-page documents to elaborate volumes, depending on the estate size and preferences of the person making the will. Wills describe the estate, the people who will receive specific property, and may even provide special instructions about care of minor children, gifts to charity, and the formation of testamentary trusts.

Who Can Make a Will?

Any person of sound mind eighteen (18) years of age or older may make a Will.

Who Needs a Will?

- Anyone over the age of 18 who owns any property (whether personal or real property).
- Single persons who want to decide for themselves where their property will go.
- Married couples to protect their surviving spouse.
- Parents to protect children and spouse.
- Grandparents to protect their children and grandchildren.

Why Do I Need a Will?

- Absent a will, state laws of intestate succession apply to the distribution of your property at death. In other words, the courts will decide where property goes based upon predetermined succession laws.
- Upon your death, your spouse or estate may have to furnish bond and pay bond premiums, which can be avoided with a will.
- Allows you to appoint a guardian whom you trust to take care of your children in your absence. The court may or may not appoint the same person. Why leave such an important decision up to a stranger in the court system?
- Allows you to select a Personal Representative to administer your estate according to your wishes.

What Are the Benefits of Having a Will?

- Assures that property will be distributed according to your wishes. Someone will inherit your property one day. You can determine who that will be.
- Allows you to appoint a Personal Representative to administer your estate.
- Allows you to appoint a Guardian for minor children.
- Allows you to appoint a Trustee for a children's trust.
- Provides for the most economical distribution of your property.
- Can reduce delay in the distribution of your estate.
- Can minimize expenses in the settlement of your estate.
- Provides a vehicle for charitable giving.
- Provides you with peace of mind that your estate affairs are in order.

Appointing a Personal Representative

A Will usually appoints a Personal Representative ("PR") to perform the specific wishes of the testator after he or she passes on. The PR need not be a relative, although testators typically choose a family member or close friend, as well as an alternate choice. The chosen representative should be advised of his or her responsibilities before the testator dies, in order to ensure that he or she is willing to undertake these duties. The PR consolidates and manages the testator's assets, collects any debts owed to the testator at death, sells property necessary to pay estate taxes or expenses, and files all necessary court and tax documents for the estate. The choice of a PR should include considerations of trustworthiness, personality, competence, integrity, willingness and ability to serve, business skills, and knowledge of the family.

Choosing a Guardian

Testators who have minor or dependent children may use a Will to name a guardian to care for their children if there is no surviving parent to do so. If a will does not name a guardian, a court may appoint someone who is not necessarily the person whom the testator would have chosen. Again, a testator usually chooses a family member or friend to perform this function, and often names an alternate. The guardian(s) should be informed that they have been chosen and they should fully understand what may be required of them. The choice of a guardian often affects other will provisions because the testator may want to provide financial support to the guardian as they are rearing the surviving children.

WILLS FAQ

1. What happens if I die without a will?

We all have a will. We either choose to create one that reflects our wishes or state laws of intestate succession apply.

Intestate succession is the statutory method of distributing an estate's assets that are not disposed of by a will. Property may pass by intestate succession where: the decedent dies without a will, the decedent's will is denied probate due to improper execution, or the decedent's will does not dispose of all of his property resulting in a partial intestacy (usually because the will contains no residuary clause).

If a person dies without a valid will, their survivors will face a complicated, time-consuming, and expensive legal process. With an intestate estate, the probate court must step in to divide up the estate using legal defaults that give property to surviving relatives. Therefore, intestacy may mean that people who would never have been chosen to receive property will in fact be entitled to a portion of the estate. Additionally, state intestacy laws only recognize relatives, so close friends or charities that the deceased favored do not receive anything.

If no relatives are found, the estate typically goes to the state government. Intestacy statutes can be quite complex which means when a person dies without a will, the lawyers are paid thousands of dollars to sort through the laws and the facts in order to distribute the property to the rightful heirs.

Of course, this is all avoided with proper estate planning in place. When made aware of the consequences of intestacy, most people prefer to leave instructions through a Last Will rather than subject their survivors and property to government-mandated division. Appendix B is a summary of estate distributions in Colorado when the decedent dies without a Last Will. An attorney in your state should be consulted regarding your local laws.

See Appendix B, Intestate Succession in Colorado, Page 162.

2. What is Probate?

Probate is the court supervised distribution of property after death. When an individual dies owning property in his or her name, that property generally must go through probate. Probate is a legal procedure that establishes ownership of property in others. The probate system is designed to ensure the validity of a will, to give notice to all possible claimants of property, and to resolve ownership disputes and rights. Probate courts also distribute property not covered by a will (intestate estates) according to legal defaults.

Procedurally, the probate court first establishes whether the deceased left a valid will. If so, the probate process guides the division of property in accordance with the Will's provisions. If the estate is intestate or if a will is found to be invalid, the probate court applies state laws to divide up the estate. The probate court then approves of the distribution, thereby finalizing the transfers of ownership.

While making a will does not prevent the need for probate, a carefully drafted will minimizes the time a Personal Representative spends in court and speeds up the distribution of property to survivors. Compared with many other states, the probate process in Colorado is relatively efficient. The average probate takes about 6 months or so. In other jurisdictions, probate can be onerous.

3. What is a Probate Asset?

Probate assets are those assets in the decedent's sole name at death, which contain no provision for automatic succession of ownership. The probate process only controls the disposition of probate assets. A few examples of probate assets include: a bank account in the sole name of the decedent, the death benefit of a life insurance policy where the decedent's estate is the named beneficiary, real estate titled in the sole name of the decedent or real estate held by the decedent as a tenant in common, investment accounts (stocks, bonds, mutual funds) where the decedent is the sole owner and no beneficiary is named (or the named beneficiary has predeceased the decedent), and retirement accounts where no beneficiary has been named (or the named beneficiary has predeceased the decedent).

At death, probate assets are transferred through the probate court according to the decedent's will, and if there is no will, according to state intestacy statutes.

4. What is a Non-Probate Asset?

Non-Probate assets are those assets which pass to beneficiaries under an instrument other than a will. Therefore, probate is not required for the property to change hands upon death. Examples of Non-Probate assets include:

- Bank Accounts (savings, checking, CD's) held as joint tenants with right of survivorship ("JTWROS") with another person.
- Investment Accounts (stocks, bonds, mutual funds) held as JTWROS with another person.
- Life Insurance Policies where a surviving beneficiary is properly named and the decedent's estate is not the named beneficiary.
- Annuities where a surviving beneficiary is properly named and the decedent's estate is not the named beneficiary.
- Retirement Accounts (IRA's, 401K's, pension plans) where a surviving beneficiary is properly named and the decedent's estate is not the named beneficiary.
- Real Estate owned by a husband and wife as JTWROS is a non-probate asset when the first spouse dies. However, it is a probate asset when the second spouse dies or where the spouses die simultaneously.

- Other contractual agreements which contain Payable on Death (P.O.D.) or Transfer on Death (T.O.D) beneficiary designations.
- Interests held in Trust such as property transferred during the decedent's life into a Revocable Living Trust or an Irrevocable Trust.

Upon the decedent's death, these assets will automatically pass to the named beneficiaries or survivor without court supervision. This is called passing "outside of the will" or passing "by operation of law." Therefore, the provisions in a will do not control the distribution of non-probate assets.

5. **Why Do I need to know the difference between Probate and Non-Probate Assets when creating my will?**

Because the provisions in a will have no bearing over the distribution of non-probate assets to your beneficiaries. This should be taken into account when you are creating your will so that your overall estate plan accomplishes your ultimate goals. As you are creating your will, you should also take steps to make sure that your non-probate property will pass according to your wishes. For bank accounts, investment accounts, life insurance policies, annuities, retirement accounts, and other T.O.D. and P.O.D. contracts, you should obtain copies of the documentation which shows how the asset is titled and who is named as the beneficiary. The beneficiary designations should reflect your wishes, while taking into account their impact on your overall estate plan.

If necessary, beneficiary designations should be changed by requesting the appropriate forms with the person/entity responsible for managing the asset (i.e., banker, employer, financial advisor, or insurance agent). Successor beneficiaries should also be named in the event that your primary beneficiary predeceases you. Beneficiary designations can typically designate that the asset be divided into fractional shares (i.e., a life insurance death benefit could pay each of your three children 1/3).

For real estate, you should obtain a copy of the deed(s) and make certain that the asset is properly titled. If not, you should seek the advice of an attorney to help you re-title the asset. If you do not have the real estate deed in your possession, you should obtain a copy from the county clerk and recorder's office in the county where the real estate is located. All non-probate assets should be properly titled and all beneficiary designations should be updated to reflect your wishes.

Additionally, you should review and update beneficiary designations if your circumstances or desires change. Failure to plan for the distribution of non-probate assets can have devastating consequences regarding taxation, equitable distribution, and family strife. Due to complex state and federal gift taxes, income taxes, and estate taxes, a CPA should be consulted anytime you are shifting or re-titling assets.

6. Can I just re-title all of my assets into joint ownership instead of creating a will?

Generally, your will only controls distribution of assets that are titled in your name alone at the time of your death. With that in mind, some people believe that placing all of their assets in joint tenancy with right of survivorship arrangements and payable on death (P.O.D.) accounts is an inexpensive way to avoid probate and the need to create a will. This type of "backyard" estate planning is never recommended, as there are numerous risks.

First, if a married couple dies in a common accident, then their spouse beneficiary is not alive to receive the property. Therefore, the property will end up passing according to state intestacy laws because the couple did not have a will in place. Likewise, if a non-spouse beneficiary predeceased the decedent, then state intestacy laws will control the distribution of property.

Secondly, holding property jointly with a child gives the child an ownership interest in the entire property. So, if you have a joint bank account with your adult child, the child can exhaust all of the funds in the account. Also, the funds are subject to the child's creditors.

Thirdly, giving joint ownership or full ownership rights to another person can cause significant federal gift tax consequences. Furthermore, if ownership is transferred for less than fair market value, then a potentially taxable gift occurs. On the other hand, a properly drawn will names your personal representative, names your guardian, avoids costly court requirements, and disposes of property according to your wishes if your spouse or beneficiaries predecease you.

A will based plan along with updated beneficiary designations on your right of survivorship and P.O.D. accounts is always the sensible choice. On the contrary, backyard estate planning offers very little (if any) reward and plenty of risks.

7. How can I change my will?

If a will is valid, it is effective until it is changed, revoked, destroyed, or invalidated by the writing of a new will. Changes or additions to an otherwise acceptable will can be most easily accomplished by adding a Codicil. A Codicil is a document amending the original will, with equally binding effect. Therefore, a Codicil must be executed in compliance with applicable law, using the same formality as the original will. Wills should not be changed by simply crossing out existing language or adding new provisions, because those changes do not comply with the formal requirements of will execution. If a change needs to be made to your will you should seek the advice of an attorney.

8. When should I consider creating a new will?

An outdated will may not achieve its original goals because its underlying assumptions may have changed. Additionally, changes in probate and tax law may change the effectiveness of certain provisions. Wills should be reviewed at least every two (2) years, as well as upon major life changes such as births, adoptions, deaths, marriages, divorces, and major shifts in a testator's property. Because state law governs wills, if a testator moves to a new state, their will should be reviewed for compliance with their new state's laws.

Additionally, wills with tax provisions may not accomplish your goals due to frequent changes in the federal estate tax laws. For example, a will with a martial formula clause which places the maximum amount allowable in a bypass trust and leaves the remainder outright to the surviving spouse may have worked well in the year it was drafted. However, with the increase in the federal estate tax exemptions, the same marital formula today may fully fund a bypass trust while leaving no assets passing to a surviving spouse outright. This could be devastating for a surviving spouse in need of cash.

9. How can I revoke my will?

A testator can revoke a will by: 1) creating a new will, or 2) by a physical act such as intentionally destroying, obliterating, burning, or tearing up the will. Changed circumstances may also revoke a will. A divorce, for example, revokes all provisions in a will in favor of the former spouse. However, the rest of the will remains valid and the will is read as if the former spouse predeceased the testator. Also, marriage plus the birth or adoption of a child revokes a pre-marital will. An attorney should be consulted when a testator desires to revoke their will.

10. Should a Trust be created in my will?

Testamentary Trusts (trusts created at death) are often utilized to distribute property to minor children in an efficient manner or to make meaningful charitable gifts.

11. Should I mention real estate in my will?

Real Estate (real property) is not typically mentioned in a will. If real estate is held jointly by husband and wife as joint tenants with right of survivorship, it will pass automatically to the surviving spouse by operation of law. Even if the will expresses something to the contrary, such property will pass automatically to the joint owner. However, property owned in the decedent's name alone and property held in a tenancy in common, are probate assets and are subject to the provisions in a will.

Unless otherwise specified, real estate subject to the provisions in a will passes according to the remainder (residuary) clause in the will (which means the primary beneficiaries named in the will receive the property). If the real property is a probate asset and the testator wants the property to pass to the residuary beneficiaries, there is no reason to specify such in the will. However, if the testator wishes to distribute the real property in a pre-residuary clause in the will to a specific individual, this option is available.

12. Can I make Specific Bequests (specific gifts) in my will?

A specific bequest is a statement in the will that a certain asset or specific amount of money will be given to a beneficiary(ies). Specific bequests may be cash, real property, motor vehicles (automobiles, tractors, recreational vehicles, etc.), stocks and bonds (assuming a beneficiary designation does not already control disposition by operation of law), and business interests (i.e., LLC membership interests or stock in a corporation).

A specific bequest may be made to an individual or to a charitable organization. However, these bequests will be distributed first and may deplete your estate if there are not enough assets in the estate to make specific bequests and residuary distributions to your ultimate beneficiaries. Also, specific bequests lapse (become null and void) if the property given cannot be found at your death, which can make the probate process more complicated.

Therefore, if you make specific bequests, only give property or amounts of cash that you are reasonably sure you will have when you die. If you make no specific bequests, all of the property will pass to your residuary beneficiaries.

13. What is meant by the Residuary or Remainder of my estate?

Your residuary estate is whatever property remains after paying debts and expenses of administration, and distribution of any specific bequests. Your residuary estate may be left to individuals, charitable organizations, or both. Because many people do not make specific bequests, the residuary usually describes all the property in your estate left to your primary beneficiaries.

TRUSTS - An Overview

Trust - A written document providing that property be held by one (the "trustee") for the benefit of another (the "beneficiary"). A trust may be created during the grantor's lifetime or after his or her death.

A trust is a legal device whereby a trustee (an individual such as a spouse, or an institution such as a bank or trust company) manages property as a fiduciary for one or more beneficiaries. The trustee holds "legal title" to the property and the beneficiaries hold "equitable title" to the property. The beneficiaries are entitled to payments from the trust income and sometimes from the trust corpus as well. Some essential trust terms are:

- **Grantor**: the grantor is also known as the trustor or settlor. The grantor is the person who transfers the trust property to the trustee.

- **Trust Property**: a trust must have property. Trust property includes assets like cash, securities, real property, tangible personal property, and life insurance policies. These assets can be either transferred during the life of the grantor ("inter vivos") or at his or her death ("testamentary"). The trust property may also be referred to as the corpus, principal, or trust res.

- **Trustee**: The trustee is the individual or entity responsible for holding and managing the trust property for the benefit of the beneficiary. Trustees can be a corporate fiduciary, professional trustee, or any competent individual who is not a minor. The trustee holds legal title to the trust property. As such, the trustee has a fiduciary duty to the beneficiaries with respect to the trust property. In the event of a breach of fiduciary duty, a trustee may be held personally liable. Such breaches include failing to pay out distributions or misappropriation of trust funds.

- **Beneficiary**: the beneficiary is the individual or entity who will receive the benefits of the trust property. The beneficiary holds the beneficial title to the trust property. The trust document must clearly identify the beneficiary or beneficiaries.

Trusts are estate planning tools that can replace or supplement wills as well as help manage property during life. A trust manages the distribution of a person's property by transferring its benefits and obligations to different people. There are many reasons to create a trust, making this property distribution technique a popular choice for many people when creating an estate plan.

Creation of a Trust

The basics of trust creation are fairly simple. To create a trust, the grantor transfers legal ownership to a person or institution (the "trustee") to manage that property for the benefit of another person (the "beneficiary"). The trustee often receives compensation for his or her management role. As stated above, trusts create a fiduciary relationship running from the trustee to the beneficiary, meaning that the trustee must act solely in the best interests of the beneficiary when dealing with the trust property.

If a trustee does not live up to this duty, then the trustee is legally accountable to the beneficiary for any damage to his or her interests. In some cases, the grantor may act as the trustee himself or herself and retain ownership instead of transferring the property, but he or she still must act in a fiduciary capacity. A grantor may also name himself or herself as one of the beneficiaries of the trust. In any trust arrangement, however, the trust cannot become effective until the grantor transfers the property to the trustee.

Testamentary and Living Trusts

Trusts fall into two broad categories, "testamentary trusts" and "living trusts." A testamentary trust transfers property into the trust only after the death of the grantor. Because a trust allows the grantor to specify conditions for receipt of benefits, as well as to spread payment of benefits over a period of time instead of making a single gift, many people prefer to include a trust in their wills to reinforce their preferences and goals after death. A testamentary trust is not automatically created at death but is commonly specified as a provision in a will. Therefore, the trust property must go through probate prior to commencement of the trust.

> *Example*: A parent specifies in her will that upon her death her assets should be transferred to a trustee. The trustee manages the assets for the benefit of her children until they reach an age when the parent believes they will be ready to control the assets on their own.

A living trust, also sometimes called an "inter vivos" trust, starts during the life of the grantor, but may be designed to continue after his or her death. This type of trust may help avoid probate if all assets subject to probate are transferred into the trust prior to death. A living trust may be "revocable" or "irrevocable." The grantor of a revocable living trust can change or revoke the terms of the trust any time after the trust commences. The grantor of an irrevocable trust, on the other hand, permanently relinquishes the right to make changes after the trust is created.

Revocable "Living" Trust

A Revocable Living Trust (RLT) is an estate planning tool that deeds property to heirs (similar to a will), but permits the grantor to retain complete control over the property during his or her lifetime. The grantor may buy, sell, make gifts, amend or even revoke the trust at any time. This means that the grantor can take back the funds placed into the trust or change the trust terms at a later date if desired. Thus, the grantor is able to reap the benefits of the trust arrangement while maintaining the ability and flexibility to change the trust document at any time prior to death.

Upon the grantor's death, the property passes to the beneficiaries, avoiding the delay and expense of probate. In the right situation, a Revocable Living Trust can be the key instrument which achieves your estate planning goals. In states such as California and Florida, the Revocable Living Trust is widely used to avoid probate due to arduous and costly probate procedures in those jurisdictions. In my state of Colorado, however, the probate process is fairly efficient. Companies that promote living trusts are responsible for much of the misinformation regarding these tools.

For example, it is a common misconception that a living trust provides better tax advantages than a will. However, both wills and living trusts can be utilized in estate tax planning, accomplishing identical tax savings. Revocable Trusts are generally used for the following purposes: asset management, avoidance of the costs and delays associated with probate, avoidance of ancillary probate if real property is owned in more than one state, avoidance of guardianship and conservatorship proceedings during incapacity, and to provide grantor(s) with a flexible estate planning tool which can be valid in other jurisdictions if moving from state to state is anticipated.

Don't get me wrong, the living trust can be extremely effective in the right situation. Whether it is right for you depends on your unique set of family circumstance and estate planning goals.

PLANNING POINT

Be leery of invitations to fancy revocable trust seminars where a free dinner is served at a swanky restaurant. These seminars are typically conducted by local financial advisors who are working with out of town attorneys. The attorney flies into town for one night only and the duo presents the Revocable Living Trust as the silver bullet for all of your estate planning needs. At the end of your fancy dinner, you are expected to pull out your checkbook and pay them several thousand dollars for their (you must be an idiot if you don't do this) estate plan. In my practice, I have seen many such documents that contain one-size fits all boilerplate language and the trusts are hardly ever funded with any assets. I have even received recorded messages during dinner time inviting me to revocable trust seminars. Let me tell you, if your estate planning process begins with a recorded sales pitch, watch out. Jesus' words in Matthew 10:16 come to mind: "...so be wise as serpents and innocent as doves." There are many advantages to using a Revocable Living Trust plan, however, they should always be fully explained by trusted, local legal counsel. Preferably counsel that is well versed in estate law and who is a member of the Christian Legal Society. In my career, I have conducted many seminars on various estate planning topics, including Revocable Living Trusts. However, these seminars are based upon educating clients on the pros and cons of estate planning techniques and allowing the client to decide which techniques fit their goals. Your estate planning goals and family dynamics should always drive your planning. Clients often end up choosing a Revocable Trust, but this should only be done after understanding this tool and considering all options.

Transferring Assets into a Revocable Living Trust

If a person transfers all of his assets into a revocable trust, he owns no assets at his death. Therefore, his assets do not have to be transferred through the probate process. Even though the grantor of the trust died, the trust did not die, so the trust assets do not have to be probated. However, trusts avoid probate only if all or most of the deceased person's assets had been transferred to the trust while the person was alive. To allow for the possibility that some assets were not transferred, most revocable living trusts are accompanied by a "pour-over" will, which specifies that at death, all assets not owned by the trustee should be transferred to the trustee of the trust.

> *Example*: John, a widower, sets up a revocable trust. It states that on his death, his assets should be distributed to his children in equal shares. John transfers his house to the trust, but does not transfer some rental real estate he owns in his name alone. At John's death, the trust can distribute the house outside of the probate process, but the rental real estate will have to go through probate. Based on the pour-over will, the probate court will order the rental real estate be transferred to the trustee, who will then distribute it according to the terms of the trust.

Thus, it is extremely important to properly fund a trust in order to avoid the probate process. It is estimated that over eighty five percent (85%) of trusts in the United States are unfunded, which means that clients pay for the benefits of a trust without actually benefitting from the arrangement. It is best to have an attorney assist the client with the funding process so that property is correctly re-titled into the trust.

Irrevocable Trust

An irrevocable living trust is an estate planning trust, wherein the grantor does not retain complete control of the assets or property. An irrevocable living trust may also be used to avoid probate. Because the grantor must permanently depart with the ownership and control of the property being transferred, such a device has limited appeal. However, irrevocable trusts are useful in life insurance planning and charitable trust planning as discussed below, particularly for larger estates facing potential estate tax liability.

TRUSTS FAQ

1. What are some of the different types of trust tools available?

Credit Shelter Trust

A Credit Shelter Trust (also referred to as a bypass trust, "B" Trust, or a family trust) is a popular estate-planning tool traditionally used to help protect assets from successive estate taxes. Credit Shelter Trust provisions may be inserted into a will or into a revocable living trust. While current laws permit an unlimited amount of assets and property to pass to a surviving spouse tax free, transfers to children and other beneficiaries valued in excess of the applicable exclusion amount ($5.43M in 2015) will be subject to federal estate taxes. A couple taking advantage of a credit shelter trust generally arranges for certain assets to pass into a trust for the benefit of a surviving spouse, rather than passing all assets directly to the spouse.

This trust, which would not be considered part of the surviving spouse's estate, may pay the surviving spouse income for life and then upon his or her death may pass to a beneficiary, such as a child, free of estate taxes if under the applicable exclusion amount (with the appreciation of the trust assets also passing estate tax free). The gross estate of the surviving spouse, upon his or her death, could also pass to the same beneficiary, meaning an additional $5.43M would be free of estate taxes. An illustration of this planning technique can be found in **Appendix C, Pages 163, 164.**

PLEASE NOTE: The American Taxpayer Relief Act of 2012 made the $5.25M Federal Estate Tax Exemption Permanent (indexed for inflation in future years). The tax rate for single person estates above $5.43M (in 2015) and married couple estates above $10.86M (in 2015) is a flat rate of 40%. Furthermore, the Act allows a surviving spouse to add to their deceased spouses exemption amount to their own exemption (which is called "portability"). Portability, in some cases, eliminates the need for complex estate planning (i.e., the use of Credit Shelter Trust language in the estate planning documents) designed to bypass federal estate taxes, which was commonplace prior to the new law.

Under the old federal estate tax laws, the exemptions were not portable, meaning that the first exemption was lost without proper estate planning through the use of Credit Shelter Trusts. Using a Credit Shelter Trust as described above may still have some estate planning benefits despite the addition of portability into the federal estate tax regime including:

1. Although the estate tax law changes were made permanent, nothing is ever really permanent in Washington, DC. Therefore, larger estates may still want to include discretionary Credit Shelter Trust language in their documents so that their estate planning is flexible enough to deal with estate tax changes that may occur in the future.

2. There are several non-tax benefits of a Credit Shelter Trust, including: asset protection, professional management of assets, and preservation of assets for children.

QTIP Trust

The entire value of an estate passing to a surviving spouse receives a marital deduction from estate taxes if the surviving spouse is a U.S. citizen and if the property passing to the surviving spouse is not a "terminable interest". If the property passes to the surviving spouse as a terminable interest, then the transfer does not qualify for the marital deduction unless technical requirements are met. A terminable interest is an interest which will terminate or fail on the lapse of time or the occurrence or failure to occur of a contingency. An interest which passes from the decedent to any other person other than their surviving spouse and such other person enjoys the interest after the termination of the spouse's interest, is a terminable interest.

For example, leaving property to a surviving spouse which terminates if the spouse remarries is a terminable interest. An exception to the terminable interest rules is a Qualified Terminable Interest Trust (QTIP). A QTIP Trust provision included in a will or Revocable Trust plan allows the testator to leave property for the benefit of the surviving spouse during their lifetime while maintaining control over where the property goes after the surviving spouse's death. If properly drafted, a QTIP election will be made by the decedent's personal representative and the QTIP will qualify for the estate tax marital deduction.

The following technical rules apply: 1) the surviving spouse must receive all of the income from the trust during their lifetime, payable at least annually; 2) no person including the spouse can appoint the income to anyone other than the spouse during the spouse's lifetime; 3) the QTIP property is included in the surviving spouses taxable estate when they die; 4) QTIP treatment must be elected by the executor of the estate upon the testator's death.

A QTIP trust can be a good option where spouses are in a

second or third marriage. For example, the surviving spouse is provided with income from the trust for life and when they die the first spouse's children from their first marriage receive the remainder of the trust. If the first spouse is concerned that their surviving spouse could disinherit their children, then a QTIP trust can be useful.

This type of trust offers many advantages, however, the testator should keep in mind that the surviving spouse looses direct control over the assets placed into the trust (though they are still entitled to income from the trust) which could be problematic if the surviving spouse will need the property outright for standard of living and cash flow purposes. Additionally, the surviving spouse is more likely to exercise their spousal elective share rights before the QTIP trust is created (See CO Revised Statutes § 15-11-201 or your state's elective share law).

Irrevocable Life Insurance Trust (ILIT)

An ILIT is a common estate-planning tool for wealthy clients, which I would categorize as clients with at least a $5.43 million estate. Typically, the proceeds from any life insurance policy owned by you are included in your estate for estate tax purposes (though they are not part of your "probate" estate assuming you have properly named a beneficiary). An Irrevocable Life Insurance Trust is a unique legal document which helps keep the proceeds of a life insurance policy outside of the estate and thus potentially free of estate tax and income tax.

The ILIT is a legal entity that becomes operational while one is still living. The trust becomes the owner of the life insurance previously owned or of a new policy purchased in the trust's name. Because the policy is owned by this legally independent trust, you would not be the legal owner of the proceeds, which therefore are not included in your taxable estate. Below are some of the potential advantages and disadvantages of using an ILIT:

Pros:

1. Removes life insurance proceeds from your taxable estate.
2. Provides tax-free liquidity (cash) to your estate.
3. Preserves real estate, family business or other illiquid assets.
4. Uses life insurance proceeds in coordination with charitable gifting in order to replace assets given to a charity.
5. Increases the size of the estate left to heirs.
6. Maximizes inheritance while minimizing taxes paid to the federal government.

Cons:

1. ILIT's can be somewhat costly to create and maintain. Costs include attorney's fees for drafting the trust, and annual professional trustee fees (approx. $1,500-$3,000) charged for drafting the required Crummey letters to the beneficiaries, paying the insurance premiums, and acting as trustee.
2. Transferring funds to the trustee to pay the insurance premiums could take up your entire annual federal gift tax exclusion of $14,000 per individual (2015) which limits other gift giving ability.
3. If you are transferring an existing life insurance policy into an ILIT and die within 3 years of the transfer, the death benefit funds from the policy will be included in your taxable estate.
4. Permanence and Loss of Control: the assets are no longer the owners once they place them in the ILIT and the trust is irrevocable.

There are two ways to establish and fund an ILIT. The

first, and best, way to do this is by establishing the ILIT first, and then allowing the ILIT to purchase the life insurance. The second method is by establishing an ILIT and contributing an existing life insurance policy to the ILIT. Establishing the ILIT first is preferable, because doing so will allow you to avoid any gift tax on the initial funding of the trust. Also, when existing insurance policies are transferred into an ILIT the benefits will be included in your taxable estate if you die within three (3) years of the transfer. You, as the Settlor, make contributions to the ILIT. The trustee then takes the contributions and uses them to pay the premiums on the life insurance policy.

In order to avoid gift tax on the contribution to the ILIT, the trust agreement must be properly drafted, and several technical steps must be followed. The policy premiums are typically paid by the Settlor in a manner that avoids gift taxes by use of the annual gift tax exclusion (currently $14,000 per year). If you have an existing policy, you may establish your Irrevocable Life Insurance Trust and contribute the existing policy to the ILIT. Doing so will result in a taxable gift, although you may use part of your lifetime gift tax credit (currently $5.43 million in 2015) to avoid paying any gift tax on the transfer. The amount of the gift will depend on whether it is a term or whole life policy.

Upon your death, the trustee of the ILIT files the claim for the death benefits. The insurance company issues the check to the ILIT, and the policy proceeds are distributed to the ILIT beneficiaries and excluded from your gross estate. The terms of the ILIT should allow the trustee to make loans to, or purchase assets from, your estate. This provides liquidity to the estate for payment of any estate taxes, and prevents a forced sale of assets which may be illiquid or assets your heirs do not wish to sell.

> *Example:* John has an estate which totals $10 million, of which $5M is a death benefit in a large life insurance policy. He will not owe any federal estate taxes on $5.43M under the 2015 Applicable

Exclusion Amount, but he will be taxed on the remaining $4.57M. Therefore, $4.57M of his estate will be subject to Federal Death Tax at a 40% rate (i.e., $1.83M in taxes). John could avoid paying any Federal Estate taxes by transferring the insurance policy into an Irrevocable Life Insurance Trust. Upon his death, the trust, as the owner and beneficiary of the policy, will collect the life insurance death benefit proceeds from the insurance company and distribute them to the named beneficiary. In this scenario, John's estate would be able to avoid paying $1.83M in taxes and this money could be used to benefit one of his family members, a friend, or a charitable organization instead of the federal government.

Charitable Remainder Trust (CRT)

A Charitable Remainder Trust can be a highly effective financial and estate planning tool. This irrevocable trust provides an income stream to the donor or to other noncharitable beneficiaries for life or for a term of years and pays the remainder interest in the trust to one or more qualified charitable organizations. A CRT can be either inter vivos or testamentary in nature, but typically they are created inter vivos (during the donor's lifetime). An inter vivos CRT is created by a written irrevocable trust agreement executed by the donor and the trustee during the donor's lifetime. A testamentary CRT is created by the donor's will or Revocable Living Trust. The pros and cons of a CRT are as follows:

Pros:

1. Allows the grantor to avoid capital gains taxes on highly appreciated assets.
2. Donor or donor's beneficiaries receive an income stream based on the full, fair market value (FMV) of those assets.

3. Donor is able to claim an immediate charitable deduction on his or her income tax return.
4. The contributed assets are removed from the donor's estate, so there is no estate tax liability on such assets and the donor's lifetime unified estate/gift tax exemption is not reduced as a result of making the gift.
5. The trust assets ultimately benefit the charity(ies) chosen by the donor.

Cons:

1. The trust is irrevocable.
2. The portion of your estate that you donate to the trust is not available to your heirs (although in combination with an irrevocable life insurance trust the wealth can be replaced with life insurance payable to your heirs).

There are two primary types of charitable remainder trusts- charitable remainder annuity trusts (CRAT's) and charitable remainder unitrusts (CRUT's).

Charitable Remainder Annuity Trust (CRAT)

The annuity trust pays a fixed dollar amount to the donor or other noncharitable beneficiaries each year, regardless of how the value of the trust may change. The fixed dollar amount is based upon a fixed percentage of the initial fair market value of the trust property. An annuity trust may last for a term of years (not to exceed 20) or for the lifetime of the income beneficiary. The income payout from a CRAT to the donor must be at least 5% but no more than 50% of the initial value of the assets transferred to the CRAT. The CRAT has one basic form - a fixed dollar amount.

Pros:

1. If the trust assets decrease in value, the annuity payments remain the same.

2. Donor receives a predictable fixed income stream for their life or a term of years.

Cons:

1. There is no protection against inflation because the annual payments are fixed. In other words, 20 years of inflation will mean that $10,000 fixed will have a lot less buying power than it does today.

2. The income stream ceases if the assets are depleted.

Charitable Remainder Unitrust (CRUT):

The unitrust pays the donor or other noncharitable beneficiaries a fixed percentage of the value of the trust property as is re-valued each year. Also, unlike an annuity trust, which may not accept further contributions beyond the initial funding, additional contributions may be made to a unitrust (assuming it is created while you are living and the payments meet specific IRS guidelines). The income payout from a CRUT to the donor must be at least 5% of the annual value of the assets in the CRUT.

Pros:

The payments to noncharitable beneficiaries are protected against inflation because the unitrust payment is based upon the value of the trust assets annually. If the assets increase in value, the unitrust payment is larger than the previous year.

Cons:

Because the assets may decrease in value from one year to the next, there is no protection against a decline in the value of the assets in the trust.

The CRUT has 4 configurations:

1. The standard fixed percentage CRUT pays a fixed percentage of the value of the trust assets, revalued annually.

2. The net income CRUT pays the fixed percentage, or all of the income earned, whichever is less.

3. The NIMCRUT pays the fixed percentage, or all of the earned income, whichever is less, with a make-up provision which allows payment shortfalls in early years to be made up in later years.

4. The Flip-CRUT first pays the fixed percentage, or all of the income earned, whichever is less, and then upon the occurrence of a specified event, flips or changes to a standard fixed percentage CRUT.

A charitable trust may be funded with a gift of cash, securities, real property or closely held business interests.

Taxes and Technical Requirements

A CRT must also meet some very specific IRS guidelines. For instance, the trust must function exclusively as a charitable trust and payments from the trust must be at least 5% but not more than 50% of the trusts value (initial FMV for an annuity trust and annual value for a unitrust). Additionally, the date of gift value of the charitable remainder interest (determined under Internal Revenue Code § 7520), must equal at least 10%

of the total value of all assets contributed to the trust at the time the contribution is made.

This rule ensures that there will eventually be a remainder gift made to the charity at the end of the trust term. CRAT's must also meet a 5% rule that says a CRAT will fail if there is more than a 5% probability, determined at the time of funding, that the trust assets will be exhausted before the end of the initial term of the trust. Charitable Remainder Trusts are pretty popular when interest rates are high, because it is much easier to meet the 10% and 5% IRS rules due to the fact that the trust assets are growing and there is a high likelihood that there will be a charitable remainder devise when the trust term is complete.

The CRT also offers the donor with several significant tax advantages. First, the trust itself if exempt from paying federal income taxes. However, the noncharitable beneficiaries must still pay income taxes at their current income tax rates when they receive annuity or unitrust payments. Secondly, the donor will receive an estate tax charitable deduction equal to the date of death value of the gift of the remainder interest to charity. Therefore, the remainder interest is removed from the donor's estate and is not subject to federal estate taxes. Thirdly, the donor will receive an income tax deduction in the year of the gift equal to the fair market value of the remainder interest passing to charity.

Example of Charitable Remainder Trust

> *Example*: Husband and Wife, a couple in their 60's, own a ski condo in Colorado. As they are getting older, they seem to be using the condo less and less. Also, the maintenance fees are now quite expensive. They have considered selling the condo, however it has a fair market value of $500,000 and they purchased it for only $150,000 twenty years ago. If they sold it, they would have to pay capital

gains taxes (up to 23.8% on the gain or approximately $83,300 in taxes).

Husband and wife are very passionate about a certain Christian University, and instead of selling the condo, choose to donate it to a charitable remainder trust. The trustee then sells the condo (tax free) and reinvests the trust assets into a diversified portfolio. Husband and wife receive a charitable income tax deduction for their gift ($145,000) and they receive an annual income of 5% of the fair market value of the trust (Charitable Remainder Unitrust is valued annually) or approximately $25,000 per year.

The value of the condo is removed from the couples taxable estate, capital gains taxes are avoided, they receive an income tax deduction for the charitable gift, and their favorite Christian University ultimately receives a sizable charitable gift that is used to advance God's Kingdom through educating the next generation of believers. If they wanted to replace this wealth and leave $500,000 to their children, the couple would simply use the income from the charitable trust to pay the premiums on a $500,000 term life insurance policy that is held in an Irrevocable Life Insurance Trust for the benefit of their children. In that scenario, the charity receives the remainder and the kids still get the $500,000.

See Appendix D, Charitable Remainder Trust, Page 165.

* The numbers used herein are for illustrative purposes only. Actual tax savings and trust income payments vary according to the client's circumstances.

> **PLANNING POINT**
>
> Donors must realize that the property donated to the Charitable Trust will ultimately pass to the qualified charitable organization and not to the donor's family. However, an ILIT can be used with a Charitable Trust as a tax-free wealth replacement tool. Basically, when the Charitable Trust pays income to the donor, the donor gifts all or part of the income to the ILIT to pay the premiums on the life insurance policy. In a nutshell, by combining the CRT and the ILIT, the donor makes a meaningful gift to charity and replaces the gift with an inheritance to the donor's family using life insurance. Ideally, if the donor makes a charitable contribution of $1 million to a trust, the donor would have the ILIT purchase a $1 million life insurance policy that would be paid to the donor's children upon donor's death. This can be a win-win-win. The donor receives the charitable benefits and income generated from the charitable trust, the charity/ministry receives the charitable remainder, and the family receives exactly the same amount of money they would have received had the charitable gift not been made.

Charitable Lead Trust (CLT)

A Charitable Lead Trust provides an income stream to one or more qualified charitable organizations for the life of a natural person or for a term of years and upon termination, distributes the remaining trust assets to the donor's non-charitable beneficiaries. A CLT is primarily used by individuals who wish to benefit a charity first, with the property ultimately passing to family members at reduced tax rates. A CLT is typically structured as an irrevocable trust during life, but it can also be created as a testamentary trust.

Pros:

1. Allows Grantor to see their charity benefit from the gift during their lifetime.
2. Leaves remaining trust assets to grantor's family at reduced transfer tax rates.
3. Substantially reduces the value of the future interest taxable gift made to noncharitable beneficiaries, essentially freezing the value of the assets.
4. If the assets in the trust outperform the IRC § 7520 rate, (the rate used by the IRS for discounting present values, annuities or future interests) the growth in the trust passes to the noncharitable beneficiaries. The IRC § 7520 rate has recently been hovering around its all-time lows. Charitable Lead Trusts are much more attractive to donors when interest rates are low, because of the potential for the invested trust assets to outperform the low rates.
5. The present value of the lead interest to charity is deductible for federal gift and estate tax purposes. A CLT can be designed to "zero out" so that the transfer of assets to heirs avoids estate and gift taxes.
6. The current economy makes Charitable Lead Trusts very attractive to wealthy donors that wish to benefit their chosen charity during lifetime.

Cons:

1. The trust is irrevocable.
2. The annual payments to charity must be made regardless of the trusts assets performance.
3. Non-Grantor CLT's are subject to income tax, but this means the trust and not the Grantor (aka Donor) is responsible for paying the annual income taxes to the IRS. Most CLT's are structured this way.

There are two types of charitable lead trusts- charitable lead annuity trusts (CLAT's) and charitable lead unitrusts (CLUT's).

Charitable Lead Annuity Trust: A CLAT pays the charity a fixed dollar amount based upon a fixed percentage of the initial value of the property. A CLAT is the most preferred CLT, because if the investments in the trust outperform the IRC § 7520 interest rate (currently at historic lows), the growth in excess of the annuity amount exclusively benefits the donor's remainder beneficiaries.

Charitable Lead Unitrust: A CLUT pays the charity a fixed percentage of the value of the trust property as is revalued each year.

Taxes and Technical Requirements

A CLT must be irrevocable and it must be set up to benefit public charities. The term of the trust may be for a certain number of years or it may be measured by the lives of certain individuals. Unlike the Charitable Remainder Trust, there is no minimum or maximum annuity or unitrust payment (i.e., CRT requires 5% to 50% annuity payment). The payments to charity must be made each year even if the trust does not generate income. Highly appreciating assets are best to fund a CLT. Even though the remainder beneficiaries will lose the step-up in basis of the assets upon the donor's death, removing the future appreciation of rapidly appreciating assets from the donor's estate often provides maximum tax benefit. Rental real estate is often a good fit for funding a CLT because it produces income for the charitable annuity payments and it will likely increase in value.

Example of Charitable Lead Trust

> ***Example:*** Henry and Mary have a high net worth and they have used up all of their lifetime gift tax

exemption ($5.43 M in 2015). They decided to contribute $1,000,000 to a CLAT that has a 20-year term and will pay 6% ($60,000) annually to a Christian ministry. Assuming the assets in the trust grow at 7% annually and assuming an IRC § 7520 rate of 1%, the IRS assumes there will be nothing in the trust after the 20-year term has ended, therefore the value of the gift to the couple's children will be calculated to be zero. In other words, the gift tax is "zeroed out." Any growth of the assets above and beyond the assumed 1% rate will pass to Henry and Mary's children. This would likely be in the hundreds of thousands of dollars with an assumed interests rate this low.

See Appendix E, Charitable Lead Trust, Page 166.

Special Needs Trusts

Planning is not optional for parents of children with special needs. It is crucial to ensure that the child will have the ordinary comforts of life that are not provided by government assistance. A special needs trust is the most effective way to provide security and quality of life for a special needs individual. A special needs trust is a legal arrangement where a trustee holds and distributes trust assets for a beneficiary who has special needs in a manner that protects the special needs child's eligibility for government provided food, clothing, and shelter benefits via Supplemental Security Income and Medicaid.

The special needs trust provides supplemental assistance for needs not already covered by government programs. A family member can often act as the trustee and use their discretion to distribute or not distribute assets for the supplemental needs of the special needs individual. Upon the death of the special needs individual, the trust assets would go to the individual's family members, friends, or perhaps a charity.

The only alternatives to a special needs trust are 1) leaving nothing to the child (see Bequeathing To Other Family Members below), 2) creating a trust that does not contain specific Special Needs Trust language (which causes the child to lose public benefits), or 3) leaving an outright inheritance to the child which disqualifies them for public benefits. None of the above are good options when compared to a Special Needs Trust. Having an older sister with special needs, I certainly understand the unique legal and personal issues associated with special needs planning.

Bequeathing to Other Family Members

While it might seem like a good idea to simply leave a set amount of money to your disabled child's sibling or other close relative, with the understanding that the money will be spent on the disabled child, this often backfires for the following reasons:

- The money can fall prey to judgments or divorce settlements against the relative, or can be lost in bankruptcy
- The relative can't be legally forced to use the money to benefit the disabled person
- The relative to whom the money is left may be taxed at a higher rate than the disabled child or a trust
- Should the relative die before the disabled child, the money would go to his or her heirs

A special needs trust avoids these potential problems without putting an emotional strain on family relations. Monthly SSI benefits can be spent on food, clothing and shelter. The special needs trust money can then go to pay for virtually any expense not met by public or private agencies such as:

- Medical and dental expenses not otherwise provided
- Education
- Training
- Rehabilitation
- Transportation (including the purchase of a vehicle)

- Life insurance premiums
- Computer equipment and electronics
- Recreation
- Vacations and airline tickets
- Summer camp

Choosing a Trustee

Anyone other than the child with special needs can serve as the trustee. The choice of trustee is one of the most important considerations that the family will face. The trustee will be responsible for custody of the trust assets as well as determining when to distribution funds for the benefit of the child.

The trustee for a special needs trust for your disabled child could be:

- A trusted family member who is close to your child
- A bank or other financial institution, who will take a percentage of the trust assets for administering the trust
- A team approach, with a financial planner and one or more family members working together as a co-trustees, or a family member as trustee with the ability to delegate the investment functions to a financial advisor
- A family friend such as special needs teacher close to the child, or your family's minister

Special Needs Trust Requirements

To be effective, a special needs trust document:

- Must have language that makes it impossible for your disabled child to demand that the trust funds be distributed
- Must give the trustee full discretion to spend the trust assets as he or she sees fit

- Must make it clear that the trust isn't intended to be a basic support trust, but that the money is intended to be used solely to supplement benefits that are otherwise available to your child
- Should specify that the trust is to be administered so that eligibility for public government assistance isn't jeopardized
- Must be managed by a trustee other than the child with special needs

Funding A Special Needs Trust

A special needs trust can be funded through a Will or gifts from relatives and friends made directly to the Trust instead of to your disabled child. Life insurance can be the most cost effective and efficient method for providing the funding necessary to establish the trust and provide for the child throughout their lifetime. It immediately places assets in the trust upon the deaths of the parents or insureds.

Letter of Intent

One way to be clear about what you intend for your disabled child's future is to make a "Letter Of Intent" to be given to his or her trustee at the time of your death. This document gives family members and others the benefit of your knowledge about your child's capabilities, needs and fears, and can be updated periodically. A letter of intent can include:

- Biographical info
- Financial details
- Medical history and needs
- Social contacts
- Any negative influences you'd like to guard against
- Personality traits
- Skills, hobbies and physical abilities
- Goals your child is working toward

Key Points

- In order to qualify for the Social Security Administration's Supplemental Security Income Benefits, ("SSI"), a disabled adult can't hold more than $2,000 in assets, excluding a car and a home. SSI benefits must be spent on food, clothing and shelter expenses.
- Eligibility for SSI makes a disabled person eligible for food stamps and Medicaid, which pays medical expenses, nursing home care and mental health services.
- As these benefits often add greatly to a disabled person's ability to care for him or herself, you wouldn't want to give your disabled child property that would disqualify him or her from receiving these benefits.
- Special Needs Trusts provide the child with money for expenses not met by public benefits.
- Special Needs Trust language is included in the parent's will or revocable trust and the trust is established upon the parent's death.
- There is no limit to the amount which can be placed in the Special Needs Trust.
- With a little planning, you can make sure that your disabled child's future will be bright, even in your absence.

Other Estate Planning Trusts Tools

Various other charitable planning tools may be considered depending on the unique needs of the client. Additionally, there are many other irrevocable trust tools and other advanced planning tools that may be useful in specific situations such as Grantor Retained Annuity Trusts, Spousal Lifetime Access Trusts, Intentionally Defective Grantor Trusts, Self Cancelling Installment Notes, Private Annuities, Qualified Personal Residence Trusts, and Dynasty Trusts. These complex arrangements should be discussed with your legal counsel. Using a trust can be an excellent method of accomplishing your long-term estate planning goals. As these trusts involve, in some cases, complicated tax laws, you should consult with your tax and legal professionals concerning your particular situation.

2. If life insurance proceeds are tax-free anyway, why might I need an ILIT?

While it is true that life insurance proceeds are not taxed as income, the proceeds of an insurance policy may be included in your gross estate for federal estate tax purposes. If you possess what the IRS terms "incidents of ownership" of the policy, the proceeds will be included in your gross estate and taxed accordingly. You possess any of these "incidents of ownership" if you are the owner of the policy, have the ability to change the policy's beneficiaries, can surrender, assign, or cancel the policy, borrow cash, surrender value, or otherwise pledge the policy, or if you own a majority of a corporation which is the owner of the policy.

This list is not all-inclusive, but simply illustrates that simply purchasing a life insurance policy will not necessarily provide tax-free benefits to your heirs. Proper drafting, funding, and administration of an Irrevocable Life Insurance Trust will allow the full face value of the policy to benefit your heirs. For estates that are close to or above the $5.43M federal estate tax exclusion, an ILIT might be a great planning tool to help you avoid federal estate taxes on your life insurance.

3. Can I be the trustee of my Irrevocable Life Insurance Trust?

This is not recommended. Being the trustee of your own ILIT will cause the proceeds of the policy to be included in your gross estate. You also should not choose your spouse as the trustee if the trust is funded with a second to die life insurance policy. A trusted family member, accountant, attorney, or financial institution may be good choices as trustee of your ILIT.

4. How does a grantor choose a trustee?

The choice of a trustee is extremely important. The trustee owes beneficiaries a fiduciary duty to act in their best interests and usually receives compensation for trust management activities, so the grantor usually wants to make this decision personally. Many grantors choose family members or close friends due to personal confidence in those individuals, but others prefer professional trustee institutions (such as attorneys, trust companies, banks, or CPA's) because of staff expertise. A grantor should consider the burden posed by the trust's administration, the compensation required by a trustee, and the particular needs of the trust. If a trustee is not specified in the trust document, then a court will appoint one, possibly choosing a trustee the grantor would not have chosen freely.

Legally, it is not necessary to notify the trustee prior to creating a trust, but a trustee may decline his or her appointment. Therefore, the grantor should choose someone who is willing to take on the required responsibilities, and should inform them of their appointment. It is advisable to choose an alternate trustee in the event the original choice is unable or unwilling to accept the trust obligations when the trust commences. Grantors may choose multiple trustees to act together in managing trusts. Co-trustees must act unanimously unless the trust expressly allows division of responsibilities. Naming a family member as a Co-Trustee and a professional trustee (i.e., bank or trust company) as the other Co-Trustee is becoming more popular for various types of trusts. This arrangement is beneficial because the family member better understands the family dynamics and the professional trustee has the skill and experience to navigate through complex trust laws.

5. What are some of the fiduciary responsibilities owed by a trustee to the beneficiaries?

The trustee has several major duties, including:

Loyalty: The greatest duty is for the trustee to be loyal to the beneficiaries. The trustee must administer the trust solely for the benefit of the beneficiaries, and provide full disclosure of his or her dealings. The trustee must deal fairly with the beneficiaries, and not manage the trust to profit his or her own financial interests (i.e., by buying stock in a company the trustee owns).

Administration: The trustee has a positive obligation to do what is necessary for the good of the trust.

Productivity: If the purpose of the trust is to maximize assets over time, the trustee owes a duty to make productive investments.

Earmark: The trustee must keep trust assets separate from all other assets, including those of the trustee, and must clearly identify those assets belonging to the trust in all dealings.

Account: The trustee must provide financial statements regarding the state of the trust.

Nondelegation: Because the trustee holds legal title, only the trustee may manage the trust. However, the trustee may delegate the investment functions of the trust.

Diversification: If the trust involves investment of assets, the trustee must diversify the trust's holdings as a prudent investor would do with his or her own money.

Impartiality: The trustee must act for the benefit of the trust as a whole, and not favor one beneficiary's interests over another's.

6. **Do I need a Revocable Living Trust as opposed to a Will?**

It depends. (Sounds like a lawyer answer doesn't it?) Some estate planners assert that everyone should have a living trust, while others believe that a will is all most people need. Before you make a decision, you should keep a few things in mind. First, the probate process in most states is relatively efficient. Although, a typical probate can last 6 months or so.

Secondly, the creation and maintenance of a living trust can be more costly than creating a will (typically 2 to 4 times the cost to create a will based estate plan), although the cost of probate will likely be avoided with a living trust. Thirdly, the living trust has several advantages over a Will. Below are the 7 advantages that I believe the Revocable Living Trust has over a Will.

Seven Reasons to Consider a Revocable Living Trust

1. Comprehensive Plan: A Revocable Living Trust is a great tool that coordinates all of your estate planning. It is a master document that allows for the centralized lifetime management of your assets and a smooth transition to beneficiaries upon your death. During your lifetime, the Grantors alone (typically husband and wife) have total control over the trust assets acting in their capacity as Trustees. The Grantors receive all of the income from the trust as trust beneficiaries and they can spend and manage the assets in any way they see fit. Upon the death of the first spouse, the surviving spouse has total control as Trustee. Upon the second death between spouses, the trust assets are distributed to the couples named beneficiaries according to the terms of the document.

2. Probate Avoidance: A properly funded trust avoids the probate court system that is necessary with a will based estate plan. A will must be admitted to the probate court in

the county where the decedent was domiciled upon their death. The court must then oversee the process that distributes the decedent's property according to the terms of the will. A RLT avoids probate on both the husband and wife's death.

Avoiding probate saves your family time and money during the estate administration process. An average probate will cost between $1,500 to $5,000 and a complex probate can cost in the tens of thousands of dollars. Not to mention, the typical probate in most states will take 6 months to settle. Which means that your beneficiaries will not be able to have access to your property until that process is completed.

Distributions from a trust can occur in as little as a couple of weeks. This is especially critical if you are a small business owner and you are passing on your business to your spouse or the next generation. Your beneficiaries can continue business operations immediately, without waiting for the courts approval. Lastly, having counseled many families through probate, I see firsthand the emotional stress that comes with that process. Many people choose to create a RLT to avoid that court process altogether.

3. Avoidance of Ancillary Probate: If you own real property in another state, a RLT can also help you avoid ancillary probate in that state as well. Real property in other states should be titled into the trust via Quitclaim Deed. The trust terms will dictate how the property is distributed upon your death.

4. Avoidance of Conservatorship & Guardianship Proceedings: If you become incapacitated, the court will have to appoint someone to be your Guardian and Conservator to make financial and personal decisions for you, absent specific legal direction. The court costs and attorneys fees to set up a Guardianship and Conservatorship can easily run $5,000 to $10,000. However, the Successor Trustee (typically your spouse) named in your RLT can act in these capacities

without court approval or oversight. Again, this is especially critical for a business owner that becomes incapacitated. The successor trustee is able to step right in, without having to seek the courts permission, and continue to run the business until the Grantor is no longer incapacitated. During incapacity, most people prefer to have their care and assets managed privately by people they know and trust, instead of having the court interfere with their private lives.

5. Flexibility: A RLT is not a state specific document and it does not have to adhere to the same execution formalities as a will, such as the requirement for the document signing to include 2 witnesses and a notary (required by most states). Therefore, if you move to another state in the future you will not need to create a new RLT. A simple amendment changing the jurisdiction is usually all that needs to be done. A will is a state specific document that may need to be completely redone if you move to another state.

6. Smooth Transition of Assets to Children: Upon the death of both spouses, the Successor Trustee of the RLT distributes trust assets to the children and/or other named beneficiaries according to the terms of the Trust. Again, this happens without court oversight and without the delays of probate. The distributions can be made outright to the beneficiaries or held in another trust, called a testamentary trust, for the benefit of children until they reach an age the you are comfortable with them receiving the funds outright. A testamentary trust for children can be created in a will as well, however, it cannot be funded until the probate creditor period (4-5 months) has elapsed. This transition can happened almost immediately with a RLT plan.

7. Privacy: Once a will is admitted to probate, it becomes public record. Because probate is a public process, this may invite disgruntled family members and the decedent's creditors to submit claims against the estate. Although a RLT cannot guarantee your privacy, as it can be contested in court, it is

certainly much more private than a will. The privacy of the document tends to reduce the risk of litigation from outlaws and in-laws coming out of the woodwork. There is certainly less of an opportunity to oppose your distribution wishes. The Trustee must still pay all just debts of the estate, however, keeping your estate affairs private puts the trustee in a better position to negotiate estate debts.

There are a few disadvantages to using a Revocable Living Trust. They are as follows:

1. Cost: The cost of a Revocable Living Trust reflects the attorney's time and expertise required to prepare the document. This typically includes consultation time to determine your specific needs, drafting the documents, reviewing the documents, properly funding the trust, and execution of the documents. In Colorado, a typical will plan for a husband and wife will cost between $500 for a very simple plan up to $2,000+ for a complex plan. An average will plan might be around $1,000. A RLT plan usually costs between $2,000 and $5,000+ depending on the complexity. The initial expense is greater than a will, but the benefits listed above must be considered. It will cost more initially to set up a well-drafted living trust than to have a will prepared. However, a true cost comparison should include not only the expense to establish the will or trust, but also what it will cost should you become incapacitated and after you die. In other words, probate costs and Guardianship/Conservatorship costs (est. $5,000 to $10,000) can be completely avoided with the RLT. When you make a true comparison of the lifetime costs, you may conclude that having a RLT actually costs less than a will.

2. Complexity: Once it is created, the RLT must be properly funded. This typically means transferring your home into the RLT via Quitclaim Deed, placing bank accounts in the name of the trust, placing investment accounts into the trust, and transferring personal property into the trust. For tax

purposes, retirement accounts are generally left out of the trust and should pass according to your beneficiary designation form for those assets. If assets are left out of the trust and they do not have a named beneficiary, a Pour-over-Will would have to be admitted to probate in order to bring that asset back under the control of the trust. This sounds complicated, but your attorney should be able to take away most of this burden by assisting you with the initial funding of the trust and by reminding you to put new assets in the trust as time goes along.

3. Creditor Claims: During the probate process, creditors who have been given notice have a 4-month window within which they can attach claims against the estate. Actual notice (usually in the form of a letter) must be given and notice must be placed in a local newspaper for three (3) consecutive weeks. However, a Trust does not have this same requirement and creditors have up to 1 year to make a claim against the estate. Just debts should always be paid, but an argument could be made that the public creditor notice requirements in the probate process actually invite creditor claims. For estates that are not worried about the decedent owing anyone money upon death, the RLT plan makes more sense.

Revocable Living Trust FAQ's

1. Do I lose control over the assets I place in a RLT?

    While you are acting as the Trustee (i.e. during your life while you have the mental capacity), you can do anything you want with the assets owned by the Trust and with the income earned by the Trust. You can buy, sell, spend, save, make gifts, put assets into the Trust, take assets out of the Trust – there are no limitations. All income is yours and is reported on your personal tax return; no separate Trust tax return is needed. There is no practical difference between assets you own personally and assets owned by your

Revocable Living Trust; when your sign your name on behalf of the Trust assets, you just add the word "Trustee" at the end.

2. Are Revocable Living Trusts just for the rich?

   No. It's not a matter of how much you own, but rather what you want your estate plan to accomplish that matters. I typically begin looking at RLT planning with clients whose net worth is $1 million and above, but this is not a hard and fast rule.

3. Do I lose my $500,000 exemption from capital gains on the sale of my personal residence?

   The IRS currently allows a married couple to exempt up to $500,000 from capital gains taxes on the sale of their principal residence. A home placed into a RLT is still eligible for the exclusion under the grantor trust rules.

4. Can I transfer my home into my RLT if it still has a mortgage on it?

   Yes. Under federal law, mortgage due-on-sale provisions are regulated by the Garn-St. Germain Depository Institutions Act of 1982 (Garn Act). The Garn Act, as interpreted by the Code of Federal Regulations, prevents a lender from enforcing a due-on-sale clause when a home is transferred to a revocable trust in which the borrower is a beneficiary and the home is occupied (or will be occupied) by the borrower.

5. What assets are placed into the trust?

   Typically your home, investment accounts, cash accounts, and personal property. Life insurance may be funded into the trust depending on the circumstances. Retirement accounts are typically not funded into the trust. A Pour-Over-Will is still needed to catch any assets that are not properly funded into the trust.

6. What is the Successor Trustees role if I become incapacitated?

   The Successor Trustee is obligated to act for your benefit, in your best interests, including maintaining your standard of living and, should you need medical care, providing funds to pay for top quality medical care.

7. Can a RLT be changed?

   Yes. The RLT can be revoked entirely or amended at any time during the Grantor's life. Typically, after a Grantor dies, the trust becomes irrevocable.

8. How are RLT's taxed?

   During the Grantor's life, the Trust itself is not taxed. The IRS considers it to be what is called a Grantor Trust and the Grantor(s) still pay the income taxes on the assets just like they did before creating the Trust. Assets transferred to the trust are not taxed for gift tax purposes.

9. Does my RLT need to be recorded anywhere?

   No. A RLT is a private document that does not need to be recorded with any court or government agency. It may, however, need to be registered once it becomes irrevocable upon the death of the Grantor.

10. Do RLT's provide protection from Creditors?

    No. This is a very common misconception. A RLT does not provide any creditor protection for the assets placed into the RLT. To be fair, assets that are held in your individual name during your lifetime and passed to beneficiaries via a Last

Will are not protected either. The only true creditor protection available comes from creating a comprehensive Asset Protection Shield™ plan. This typically involved the use of LLC's and domestic asset protection trusts. All high net worth clients should strongly consider an Asset Protection Shield™ plan for ultimate peace of mind. For more info, see the Asset Protection info at:
www.VeritasLawColorado.com

The Key Takeaways:

- A living trust document has more provisions than a will because it deals with issues while you are living and after you die, while a will only deals with issues that occur after your death.

- A properly prepared and funded living trust will avoid court proceedings at incapacity and death. A will provides no such protection and can, in fact, ensure court intervention at both events, which can be very costly (in time, privacy and dollars) to your family.

Conclusion:

Contrary to popular belief in legal circles, the RLT is not the silver bullet for all estate plans. Clients should become educated on the pros and cons of having a Will based estate plan vs. a Trust based estate plan. At that point it is up to the client to decide which document and fee structure they are comfortable with. The Will vs. Revocable Trust debate is usually decided on a cost benefit analysis. I have found that estates at or near $1 million begin to benefit from the cost of RLT planning, although that is not a hard and fast rule. I have had clients well under $1 million create an RLT plan and I have had clients well over $1 million create a will based plan. I just happen to think that larger estates begin to benefit from the centralized structure and privacy that the Revocable Living Trust provides.

GENERAL ESTATE PLANNING FAQ

1. **Will my family have to pay Estate ("death") Taxes when I pass away?**

On January 1, 2013, with their toes just over the edge of the fiscal cliff, Congress passed the American Taxpayer Relief Act of 2012. From an estate tax standpoint, the Act appears to be aptly named as it does provide "permanent" tax relief for most American families.

Below are a few of the key provisions of the Act regarding estate planning:

   1. **$5M Estate Tax Exemption Remains.** Each taxpayer will retain a $5,000,000 exemption from estate, gift, and generation skipping transfer tax. The $5M is indexed for inflation, which means that the inflation-adjusted exemption is $5.25M in 2013, $5.34M in 2014, $5.43M in 2015, and approximately $5.66M in 2016. These figures would be doubled for a married couple, which means in 2015, a couple could leave $10.86M to their heirs estate tax free.

   2. **Top Marginal Rate Increases.** The top estate, gift, and GST rate is increased from 35% to 40%. The increased rate should give individuals whose estates exceed $5.43M and married couples whose estates exceed $10.86M, additional motivation to implement advanced estate planning strategies in order to reduce their tax burden.

   3. **Portability of Exemption Between Spouses Remains.** Portability of the estate tax exemption between spouses has been extended permanently. Portability allows a surviving spouse to transfer their deceased spouse's unused estate tax exemption to the surviving spouse. In order to preserve their right to portability, the surviving spouse must file a Form 706 (United States

Estate Tax Return) tax return even if there is not any estate tax due.

4. Income & Capital Gains Tax Increases. The rate for long-term capital gains will remain at 15% with the addition of a new 20% rate for single taxpayers with taxable income above $400,000 or $450,000 for married couples filing jointly. Individual income tax rates will remain the same, with the addition of a new 39.6% tax bracket for single taxpayers with taxable income above $400,000 or $450,000 for married couples filing jointly.

5. Major Transfer Tax Changes Avoided. The Act avoided the fiscal free-fall associated with 1) a return to the $1M exemption for estate, gift, and GST tax; 2) the "clawback" of previous gifts where the estate tax exemption is lower than a prior gift; 3) de-unification of the estate, gift, and GST exemptions; and 4) the loss of portability.

Federal Estate "Death" Taxes: In general, when an individual passes away, the transfer of assets to his or her beneficiaries will be taxed. This is called the estate tax. Recent tax law changes which are favorable to tax payers will result in even fewer Americans being subject to this tax. The Act allows each individual to transfer up to $5.43M at death estate tax free, or $10.86M per couple. The tax rate for estates above $10.86M is a flat rate of 40%. Furthermore, the Act allows a surviving spouse to add to their deceased spouses exemption amount to their own exemption (which is called "portability"). The additional federal estate tax deductions below also apply under the new law:

- **The Marital Deduction** - You can leave an unlimited amount to a surviving spouse resulting in a 100% deduction (and no estate tax due) for those assets left to a spouse.
- **The Charitable Deduction** - You can leave an unlimited amount to a tax-exempt charity resulting in a 100% deduction (and no estate tax due) for those

assets left to charity.
- **The Applicable Exclusion Amount** - As mentioned above, you can also leave assets to any other person or entity without paying estate tax so long as the total amount of all non-spouse, non-charity bequests are less than the applicable exclusion amount available in the year of your death. Under current law, the amount is $5.43M. A table showing the applicable exclusion amounts can be found below.

State Estate & Inheritance Taxes: Most states do not have estate or inheritance taxes. However, as of this writing, the following states do: WA, OR, NE, MN, IA, IL, KY, TN, PA, NY, ME, VT, MA, RI, CT, NJ, DE, MD, DC, and HI. An analysis of such laws is outside the scope of this book. If you live in any of those jurisdictions, local legal counsel will be critical to the success of your estate plan. As of December 31, 2004, Colorado does not have a state Inheritance Tax, Gift Tax, or Estate Tax. However, the Federal Estate Tax still applies to estates that are above the exemption amounts explained below.

Under the current law, if your total taxable estate (including stocks, bonds, real estate, business interests, life insurance, personal property, retirement plans, etc.) exceeds the $5.43 million applicable exclusion equivalent, your estate will be subject to federal estate taxes at a rate of 40%. However, there are many advanced planning strategies available to help you minimize estate taxes.

See Appendix F, Federal Estate Tax Chart, Page 167.

Key Points:
- $5.43M per person total Gift and Estate Tax Exemption, or $10.86M per married couple in 2015.
- The Gift and Estate Exemptions are combined for a unified credit of $5.43M and the estate exemption is reduced by the amount of lifetime taxable gifts. In

other words, if $1M was used to make lifetime gifts, then only $4.43M would be available under the estate tax exemption.
- Portability Applies to the Gift and Estate Tax Exemption.
- Portability is not automatic. The executor of the deceased spouse must file an estate tax return within 9 months of death to qualify.
- The Act reinstates stepped up basis for assets passed to heirs. Therefore, for income tax purposes, the heirs cost basis of inherited property gets adjusted to the fair market value on the date of the owner's death (which limits capital gains taxes).
- Unlimited Marital Deduction and Unlimited Charitable Deductions still apply.
- Less than 1% of Americans will pay any Federal Estate Taxes upon death.

Many state and federal tax regulations impact estate planning, but a carefully crafted estate plan can reduce the tax burden on an estate and the survivors. Both state and federal rules and regulations are extremely complex and the advice of an estate planning attorney and tax professionals regarding tax savings is essential. A general understanding of estate taxes is necessary for any client with significant assets.

2. **What are some techniques that can be used to reduce or eliminate Federal Estate Taxes?**

Most Americans will not be subject to federal estate taxes due to the increased applicable exclusion amount of $5.43 million per person. However, some higher net worth estates could be subject to taxes. Your taxable estate is probably more than you realize (Remember- life insurance proceeds will be included in your taxable estate regardless of who the beneficiary is unless the policy is owned by an irrevocable trust). Below are a few of the techniques that can be used to reduce or eliminate your estates tax burden. Other trust techniques mentioned in the

FAQ "What are some of the different trust tools available?" (See p. 41) can also be used for larger estates.

Gifting: Clients may wish to keep their taxable estate below the $5.43 million threshold by taking full advantage of the gift tax exceptions, including 1) giving away portions of the estate in the form of annul gifts that are less than the applicable exclusion of $14,000 per individual 2) paying educational expenses for a family member or friend directly to the educational institution 3) giving a portion of the estate outright to a qualified charitable organization during the life of the donor, or 4) making a charitable contribution in their Will or Revocable Trust 5) Utilizing a Charitable Remainder or Lead Trust.

For the Christian Estate Plan, a gifting strategy not only accomplishes tax savings, but it benefits the Kingdom of God as well.

Credit Shelter Trust: Including a discretionary credit shelter trust provision in the estate planning documents could still be a good idea for some clients with larger estates. Although the $5.43M federal estate tax exemption is portable between spouses (allowing a couple to pass $10.86M to heirs estate tax free, indexed for inflation for years beyond 2015) it could still be a good idea to include this provision in your documents for a couple of reasons. First, although the new tax act makes exemption portability permanent, nothing is ever permanent in Washington and it certainly does not hurt to have this language in your document. Even if you never have the need to fund a credit shelter trust for tax purposes, it could be a good safety net in case of changing tax laws in the future. Additionally, portability is not automatic. If the surviving spouse fails to file Form 706 with IRS within 9 months of their spouses' death, they will not be able to preserve their right to use the $5.43M exemption of their deceased spouse.

Secondly, the future growth of assets in placed into a credit shelter trust will avoid further estate taxes on those assets. The downside to using this type of trust, is that the assets in the trust will not receive a step-up in basis for capital gains tax purposes on the second spouses death. If assets passed from husband to surviving wife outright on the first death (with wife filing Form 706 to exercise the portability of his exemption of course), his assets would receive a step up in basis at that time and upon the wife's death, the assets would receive another step up in basis.

> *Example* **(for a high net worth couple):** John dies leaving Mary $5.43M of assets he owned in his name alone. Mary already had $5.43M in her name prior to John's death. Mary could take John's assets outright and file Form 706 with the IRS to preserve her right to use John's exemption upon her death which would keep all $10.86M of the combined estate free from estate tax liability and the assets would receive a full step up in basis (allowing the kids to sell the assets without paying capital gains taxes).
>
> This plan is simple and effective thanks to the new federal estate tax laws. However, let's assume Mary is going to live another 10 years past John's death. If the total combined assets grow from $10.86M to $20M, Mary's estate now has to pay taxes on the $20M. Let's assume that Mary's exemption from estate taxes is now $7M (because the current $5.43M exemption is indexed for inflation in future years). Plus she gets to exclude John's $5.43M that she claimed via estate tax portability by filing the 706 on his death. That would mean $12.43M is exempt from federal estate tax. However, the assets are now $20M. Therefore, $7.57M ($20M-$12.43M exempted) is now subject to federal estate tax at a 40% rate. That would mean that Mary's estate would owe the federal government a little over $3M in taxes.

What if John's will or revocable trust included a Discretionary Credit Shelter Trust provision? In that scenario, upon John's death, Mary would fund the trust with John's $5.43M exemption and the trustee (likely Mary), would use the trust for her benefit during her life (she is entitled to income, up to 5% of the principal annually, and principal for her health, education, maintenance, and support). Upon her death, the trust assets pass to a beneficiary, such as their children, free of estate taxes, with the appreciation of the trust assets also passing tax-free. Assuming the total estate doubled (including the assets in the credit shelter trust) the tax savings to Mary and John's family would be significant. Again assuming a $20M total taxable estate and an inflation adjusted $7M exemption for Mary, John's original $5.43M exemption placed into the trust grew to double its original amount to $10.86M (remember the growth in the trust is estate tax free), the estate would now pay taxes on only $2.14M for a total tax of $856,000. This strategy saved John and Harry's kids a total of $2.14M in federal estate taxes. To take this one step further, Mary might consider gifting $2.14M (the amount of taxable dollars in her estate) during her lifetime to a Charitable Remainder Trust. This would give her income for life which she could use to pay insurance premiums to an Irrevocable Life Insurance Trust to benefit her kids. Upon her death, Mary's estate would owe zero estate taxes, her chosen charity will benefit from the remainder interest in the CRT, and Mary and John's kids will receive the life insurance death benefit payout. As you can see, a proper estate plan not only preserves wealth, but it can create more wealth and opportunities for philanthropy.

> **PLANNING POINT**
>
> Considering the ever-changing estate tax landscape, flexibility is the key to creating an estate plan that can accomplish your wishes regardless of future tax law changes. For most large estates, including discretionary Credit Shelter Trust language in your Last Will or Revocable Trust may still be a good idea. Discretionary Credit Shelter Trust language in your estate plan gives the surviving spouse the option (but not the obligation) to fund a trust for tax avoidance purposes based upon their income needs and the current laws. <u>Appendix B</u> will give you a visual of this type of plan.

College Savings Plan: Section 529 of the Internal Revenue Code affords a taxpayer with an opportunity to establish a special account for the purpose of paying higher education expenses. Investments in a 529 Plan accumulate income tax free and distributions used for qualified education expenses are not subject to federal income tax. One common technique used to reduce the size of taxable estate involves "frontloading" gifts to a 529 education savings plan. You can make five years worth of annual exclusion gifts ($70,000 as an individual or $140,000 per couple) to a 529 plan in 2015 for the benefit of any one person, but annual exclusion gifting to that person over the next four years will be reduced by $14,000 per year. Qualified higher education includes anything past high school, meaning college, grad school, or trade school would all qualify. Furthermore, the person who makes the gift owns the account and has control over it. The owner can change the beneficiaries at will and can even get to the money during an emergency if they are willing to pay a penalty.

Example: Grandpa and Grandma want to reduce their $10.86 million taxable estate because they are right at the federal estate tax threshold. Grandpa and Grandma set up a 529 plan and frontload their gifts to the plan for the benefit of their 4 young grandchildren. Using both of their 5 year frontloading gifts the couple is able to fund the 529 with $140,000 per grandchild or $560,000 total. The gifts will grow tax-free and be available to pay for the grandchildren's post high school education. Grandma and Grandpa could get to the money if it was absolutely necessary, but they would have to pay penalties to do so. However, that safety net is there if they need it. Now suppose one of the grandkids goes to 2 years of junior college and one wants to go to medical school. The donors can give the remaining money in the account of one of the beneficiaries to another beneficiary who is continuing their studies. The couple here has reduced their federal estate tax liability to zero and they have provided for their loved ones education. The flexibility and tax free benefits of the 529 College Savings Plan make it a great estate planning tool.

Family Limited Liability Company: A Family Limited Liability Company (FLLC) is an estate planning device which is commonly used to eliminate or minimize estate taxes. In a FLLC, the senior generation (parents) transfers valuable assets (such as investment real estate) into the entity in exchange for membership interests in the company. The junior generation (children) are given membership interests in the company as a result of a gift from the senior generation or by transferring their own assets into the company in exchange for such membership interests. The senior generation can use annual exclusion gifting ($14,000 per person or $28,000 per married couple) to transfer their wealth during their lifetime to the junior generation via membership interests in the family controlled company. There are a couple of reasons for creating a FLLC. First, when the senior generation passes away, their property which has been converted to membership interests in the FLLC will receive a valuation discount for estate tax purposes. Due to a lack of control rights and the lack of marketability associated with membership interests which are restricted to family ownership, the value of the interests owned by the senior generation are discounted for estate tax purposes. Secondly, the FLLC provides a legal structure for transferring wealth from one generation to the next. If drafted properly, the value of the membership interests transferred to the junior generation will not be included in the taxable estate of the senior generation. The FLLC can be a powerful tool used to reduce or avoid federal estate taxes.

Conservation Easements in Estate Planning: A conservation easement is a legally enforceable land preservation agreement between a landowner and a qualified land protection organization (often called a "land trust" or "land conservancy"), for the purposes of conservation. It restricts real estate development, commercial and industrial uses, and certain other activities on a property to a mutually agreed upon level. The activities allowed by a conservation easement depend on the landowner's wishes and the characteristics of the property. In some instances, no further development is allowed on the land. In other circumstances, development is allowed, but the amount and type of development is restricted by the terms of the agreement. Conservation easements may be designed to cover all or only a portion of a property. Every easement is a unique document, tailored to a particular landowner's goals and their land. The decision to place a conservation easement on a property is strictly voluntary. The restrictions, once set in place, "run with the land" and are binding on all future landowners. After the easement is signed, it is recorded with the County Clerk and Recorder and it becomes a part of the chain of title for the property. The primary purpose of a conservation easement is to protect agricultural land, timber resources, and/or other valuable natural resources such as wildlife habitat, clean water, clean air, or scenic open space by separating the right to subdivide and build on the property from the other rights of ownership. The landowner who gives up these development rights continues to privately own and manage the land and receives a charitable deduction on their federal income taxes (which may be applied over a period of several years). Additionally, the property owner may benefit from reduced property taxes and estate taxes. If granted during lifetime, the easement significantly reduces the value of the property for estate tax valuation purposes and a portion of the land value may be excluded from the gross estate altogether. Perhaps more importantly, the landowner has made the decision to be a good steward of their natural resources, preserving the conservation values associated with their land for future generations. Conservation easements are particularly useful for families looking to pass along a family farm to their heirs in a tax efficient manner. In a state with rich natural resources like Colorado, the conservation easement is becoming a poplar estate planning tool. Because conservation easement negotiation and conservation easement drafting can both be quite complex, both the land trust and the landowner are typically represented by legal counsel. An attorney can walk clients through the conservation easement process, negotiate the terms of the agreement, and helps clients identify a qualified land protection organization who will accept and enforce the easement.

3. What are Gift Taxes and Generation Skipping Taxes?

Gift Taxes

The gift tax is a tax on the transfer of property by one individual to another while receiving nothing, or less than full value, in return. The tax applies whether the donor intends the transfer to be a gift or not. The gift tax applies to the transfer by gift of any property. You make a gift if you give property (including money), or the use of or income from property, without expecting to receive something of at least equal value in return. If you sell something at less than its full value or if you make an interest-free or reduced-interest loan, you may be making a gift. Gift taxes are paid by the donor of the gift. The donor must file a gift tax return with the IRS when a taxable gift has been made. There is not a limit on how much a person can give to others during their lifetime, but a gift to an individual that is more than $14,000 (2015) in a year must be reported to the IRS in the form of a gift tax return. Additionally, any amount above $14,000 will be counted against a $5.43 million lifetime federal gift tax exclusion and the estate tax applicable exclusion amount (unified $5.43 million in 2015, discussed above) available to the individual will be reduced by the lifetime gift tax exclusion used. The $14,000 figure is an annual exclusion from the gift tax reporting requirement. This means that you may make an annual gift of $14,000 to each individual of your choice without reporting the gifts to the IRS. If you are married, both you and your spouse can separately give gifts valued at up to $14,000 (collectively $28,000) to the same person without making a taxable gift. The general rule is that any gift is a taxable gift. However, there are many exceptions to this rule. The following gifts are not taxable gifts:

1. Gifts that are less than the annual exclusion for the calendar year ($14,000 in 2015, discussed above)
2. Tuition or medical expenses you pay directly to a medical or educational institution for someone else
3. Gifts to your spouse
4. Gifts to a political organization for its use
5. Gifts to qualified charities

Concerning education and medical expenses, federal tax law allows an individual to pay for another's tuition or medical expenses above and beyond the annual exclusion amount and there is no limit on the amount that can be given for these purposes. The payments, however, must be made directly to the medical or educational institution, rather than to the recipient of the gift. Educational gifts must be applied specifically towards tuition. Payments cannot be used for room, board, books or other ancillary education expenses. Tuition payment applies to any level of schooling from nursery school to graduate school. The student may be enrolled full or part-time. Additionally, the exemption is not limited to traditional academic institutions such as colleges and universities. Any educational organization with a regular faculty, curriculum, and a student body will generally qualify. The following examples should clarify how the federal gift tax works.

> **Example 1:** In 2015, you give your daughter a cash gift of $10,000. It is your only gift to her that year. The gift is not a taxable gift because it is less than the $14,000 annual exclusion. No gift tax return needs to be filed.

> **Example 2:** In 2015, you and your spouse give your son $28,000, your daughter $28,000, and your grandson $28,000. It is your only gift to each of them that year. None of the gifts are taxable because the gifts to each individual do not exceed the annual gift tax exclusion (husband and wife combined their $14,000 annual exclusions). No gift tax returns need to be filed.

> **Example 3:** In 2015, you pay the $30,000 college tuition of your friend directly to his Christian college. Because the payment qualifies for the educational exclusion, the gift is not a taxable gift. No gift tax return needs to be filed.

> **Example 4:** In 2015, a single mom gives her 25 year old son $25,000. The first $14,000 of the gift is not subject to the gift tax because of the annual exclusion. The remaining $11,000 is a taxable gift. Due to the $5.43 million lifetime gift tax exclusion, the mom will likely never have to pay gift taxes on the remaining $11,000. However, a gift tax return must be filed with the IRS and the mom's

applicable exclusion for estate tax purposes will be reduced by the amount of the taxable gift.

Annual Exclusion Gifting

For clients who are trying to reduce the size of their taxable estate, an aggressive gifting plan which utilizes the annual gift tax exclusions can be a great way to reduce estate tax liability while providing gifts for family, friends, and charity while the donor is still alive.

> **Example:** Grandpa and Grandma have a combined taxable estate of $10.86 million. They do not want their heirs to pay any Federal Estate Taxes when the second spouse passes away. In order to reduce their taxable estate to an amount which is below the $10.86 million combined Tax Exemption, the couple decides to adopt an aggressive gifting plan. In 2015, they use their combined annual gift tax exclusions to give $28,000 to their son and $28,000 to their daughter. In that same year, they also pay tuition payments of $25,000 directly to a Christian college for each of their 6 grandkids who attend that college ($150,000 in total tuition payments for the year 2015). In 2015 they are able to give total gifts of $206,000 without the need to file any gift tax returns with the IRS. Grandpa and Grandma have kept their total estate below the $10.86M threshold, kept both of their federal estate tax exemption amounts fully intact, helped further their grandchildren's Christian education and they have helped their loved ones in a significant way while they are still alive. In order to keep their estate below the estate tax threshold, Grandpa and Grandma will want to monitor the growth of their estate and continue to make future non-taxable gifts in order to compensate for the inflation and growth. They will likely want to

continue this strategy every year. Furthermore, they may also want to gift $28,000 to a mutual fund for each grandchild on an annual basis. This would 1) utilize their annual exclusion gifts and 2) transfer the future growth of these assets out of their estate and into an account that will grow for the grandkids benefit.

Generation-Skipping Transfer Tax (GST)

The generation-skipping transfer tax is a flat tax applied to estates in addition to income, estate, and gift taxes. The tax is imposed on a transfer (either a gift during life or a transfer at death) to a person two or more generations below the transferor. A person two or more generations below the transferor is referred to as a "skip person". Grandchildren and nonrelatives 37.5 years younger than the transferor are considered skip persons by the IRS. There are several exclusions from GST. First, each transferor is granted an exemption on generation-skipping transfers. The exemption is $5.43M in 2015 (see Figure 2.3 above). Secondly, transfers under I.R.C. § 2503(e) for medical or educational expenses are excluded. Thirdly, annual exclusion gifts of $14,000 or less (subject to adjustment annually for inflation) are excluded. Lastly, the predeceased parent exception allows a grandparent to make a transfer to their grandchild free from GST where the grandchild's parent (i.e., grandparent's child) has predeceased them.

4. What do clients need to do now that the American Taxpayer Relief Act of 2012 has passed?

    1. **Review Your Estate Plan.** An estate plan is similar to a vehicle. In order to make sure that it will reach its destination, you need someone (i.e., your attorney) to look under the hood every once in a while and make sure everything is working properly. This is especially true now that we have new estate tax laws.

2. Revise Wills with Formula Provisions. Now that there is at least some predictability to the estate tax laws, tax formulas in wills with A-B Trust provisions are likely no longer necessary, and in many cases can have adverse effects on an estate plan. This is especially true if the funding of the A-B Trusts are mandatory and not discretionary. Estate plans should be revised if they contain tax formula clauses.

3. Consider Adding a Disclaimer Trust Provision. Larger estates that are still under the Estate Tax Exemption amount ($5.43M) may want to consider substituting a disclaimer trust provision for their old A-B Trust provision. A disclaimer trust provides the greatest level of flexibility to take into account the possibility of future changes to the Estate Tax Exemption, while giving the surviving spouse maximum discretion regarding the funding of a trust for their benefit.

4. Create An Estate Plan If You Don't Have One. It is estimated that over 70% of Americans do not have a basic estate plan in place. Now that the estate tax is settled for the foreseeable future, estate planning for the majority of clients has been greatly simplified. The desire to get your "affairs in order" and to make sure that your loved ones are taken care of will now take precedence over avoiding the long arm of good old Uncle Sam. Non-tax aspects of planning such as wealth distribution, asset management for minor and special needs children, asset protection, and charitable giving should be the primary focus of clients. Considering the favorable new tax laws, there has never been a better time to plan.

5. File Form 706 Upon the Death of a Spouse. Within 9 months of the death of a spouse, the surviving spouse should file Form 706 with the IRS (even if no tax is due) in order to take advantage of the portability function of the new law and preserve their right to claim their deceased spouse's unused Federal Exemption.

6. **Continue To Make Gifts.** In 2015, individuals can continue to gift up to $14,000 per year, per individual (or $28,000 per married couple), without having to file a federal gift tax return. Furthermore, the lifetime gift tax exclusion has been increased from $5.25M in 2013 to $5.43M in 2015, offering clients who maxed out their lifetime gift exclusion in 2013 the ability to make additional lifetime gifts in 2015 and beyond as the exclusion increases with inflation.

7. **Consider a Charitable Trust.** For individuals who want to leave a legacy through charitable giving, there are a variety of planning tools available. One such tool that can be particularly effective in a low interest rate environment is the Charitable Lead Annuity Trust ("CLAT"). A CLAT combines philanthropy with tax planning through the creation of an irrevocable trust that pays a charity or charities a specified annuity payment for a fixed term. At the end of the term, the remaining assets in the trust pass to the donor's noncharitable beneficiaries (typically children). A CLAT is primarily used by individuals who wish to further the work of a charity that they believe in, with the added benefit of ultimately passing on their assets to family members at reduced tax rates.

5. How can a person leave property to minor children?

Generally, the law requires that adults manage children's inheritances until the children turn eighteen. If a testator wants to leave property to children, it makes sense to name an adult to manage that property. Otherwise, a court will name someone to safeguard the property, a procedure that may delay the speedy transfer of assets. There are several ways a will or revocable can provide for property management while heirs are underage, including:

1. **Trusts:** A will or revocable trust can establish a trust

to handle property left to children. A trustee is named to manage the property for the children's benefit, and distribute trust property according to the testator's instructions. A will or revocable trust can either set up an individual trust for each individual child, or a pot trust that covers multiple children. The trustee usually follows instructions to spend trust funds to meet children's needs until they come of age. When the child or youngest child covered by the trust reaches eighteen or another given age, the trust funds are usually distributed amongst the beneficiaries and the trust ends. A trust for minors can be very flexible. For example, the testator can specify that the children are to receive 1/3 of the trust principal at the ages of 21, 25, and 30. Or the trust may specify that all of a child's share of the trust principal be distributed to any child who is 21 years of age. Due to its flexibility, most clients prefer setting up a trust for minors as opposed to allowing transfers under the statutory guidelines of the Uniform Trust to Minors Act. For more information on adding a trust form minors clause to your will, please review "How do I choose a trustee for my children's trust" below.

2. Uniform Transfers to Minors Act (UTMA) Custodians: The UTMA is a law that exists in almost every state, and gives a testator the ability to choose a custodian to manage property left to a child. If at the testator's death, the child is a minor, the custodian will manage the property until the child reaches the statutory age of twenty-one (21). At that age, the child receives whatever is left of the property outright. Unlike a trust, the testator cannot change the age at which the child receives this distribution.

3. Property Guardian: A will can name a property guardian for a child. At the testator's death, if the child is still underage, the probate court will appoint the chosen guardian to manage property for the child. At age 18, the child receives the property outright and without restrictions.

6. **How do I choose a Trustee for my children's trust?**

The choice of a trustee is extremely important. The trustee owes beneficiaries a fiduciary duty to act in their best interests and usually receives compensation for trust management activities, so the grantor usually wants to make this decision personally. Many grantors choose family members or close friends due to personal confidence in those individuals, but others prefer professional trustee institutions (such as attorneys, trust companies, banks, or CPA's) because of staff expertise. A grantor should consider the burden posed by the trust's administration, the compensation required by a trustee, and the particular needs of the trust.

If a trustee is not specified in the trust document, then a court will appoint one, possibly choosing a trustee the grantor would not have chosen freely. Legally, it is not necessary to notify the trustee prior to creating a trust, but a trustee may decline his or her appointment. Therefore, the grantor should choose someone who is willing to take on the required responsibilities, and should inform them of their appointment. It is advisable to choose an alternate trustee in the event the original choice is unable or unwilling to accept the trust obligations when the trust commences.

7. **What is a Spousal Elective Share?**

Under C.R.S. § 15-11-201, a surviving spouse may elect against his or her share under the decedent's will, or their intestate share if there is no will. The elective share is a statutory minimum entitlement of the surviving spouse. If the surviving spouse elects to exercise this right, they will be entitled to an amount equal to the value of the decedent's augmented estate multiplied by a percentage which is based on the number of years of marriage. Therefore, a surviving spouse may demand a larger distribution of their deceased spouse's estate, even if the decedent wanted them to have a smaller share. All states have similar laws. The elective share percentage in Colorado is determined as follows: ***See Appendix G, Page 168.***

8. **Who should be the beneficiary of my IRA?**

Tax deferred accounts such as IRA's consist of money which has not been subject to federal income taxes. Therefore, when funds are distributed from the IRA to the participant or to the plan's beneficiaries upon the participant's death, federal income taxes will be assessed. A surviving spouse can roll over the IRA into their own IRA in order to defer the distribution income taxes and a non-spousal designated beneficiary can roll over the IRA into an Inherited IRA, thereby deferring the distribution income taxes. The period for deferral varies depending on the specific circumstances. Additionally, an IRA roll over must occur within 60 days of the participant's death in order to meet the IRS guidelines. If the estate of the participant is the named beneficiary, income taxes will be due upon death. A trust may also be named beneficiary of the IRA and the trust can defer income taxes, however, very technical rules must be followed in order to do so.

So, who should you name as beneficiary of your IRA? A spouse is typically the best choice with children being named as contingent beneficiaries. A charity would be a good choice if a spouse and/or children are not named. A charity could also be given a percentage (i.e., 10%) with the remaining balance in the IRA passing to family. Your estate would be the next best choice. A trust would be the last option. IRA participants should consult with their financial advisor to make sure that their beneficiary designations on the plan reflect their wishes, and they should review the beneficiary designations regularly.

9. **What is a Financial Power of Attorney?**

A financial durable power of attorney is a document which authorizes an "agent" or an "attorney-in-fact" to make financial decisions on your behalf, particularly when you are not able to do so yourself. A durable power of attorney can be effective upon execution or it can be a "springing" power of attorney to be triggered only in the event of the client's incapacity. Creating a durable power of attorney for financial decisions avoids the possibility of the court system appointing a conservator to make decisions for you during incapacity. You and not the court system get to decide who will make important choices for you when you are not able to make them yourself. Every adult should have a financial power of attorney.

10. Where should I keep my estate planning documents once they have been signed?

The original will or revocable trust should be kept in a safe place so that it will not get lost or harmed by fire or weather, such as in a fireproof safe or a safe-deposit box. Additionally, the testator should leave readily available instructions to the Personal Representative or Trustee regarding the whereabouts of the originals. For example, a notation can be placed on any copies of a will stating the location of the original will. The PR and Successor Trustee should also be fully informed (either in writing or orally) of the location of safe deposit boxes and they should be given the codes necessary to access a fireproof safe. Financial Power of Attorney documents should also be kept in a safe place such as a fireproof safe or a safe-deposit box. Furthermore, you should inform your attorney in fact(s) of their appointment. A copy of your Medical Power of Attorney should typically be given to your physician and to your named agent.

11. Should I include funeral instructions in my will or revocable trust?

Funeral instructions and instructions for the disposition of last remains should not be included in your will or trust. Instead, a separate writing with such instructions should be created by you and your personal representative should be informed of its whereabouts. If you already know the funeral director you would prefer, you should consider giving the funeral director a copy of your instructions.

12. Can I find a service that is cheaper than meeting with an attorney to prepare my estate plan?

Sure you can, however, it is often true that you get what you pay for. Attorneys are licensed professionals who provide high quality legal document preparation and legal advice. There are countless do it yourself estate document prep websites and software programs (i.e., LegalZoom®, RocketLawyer®, Quicken® Willmaker, etc.), however, there is no substitute for competent and state licensed legal counsel. A software program may be able to spit out a document, but without legal counsel and a complete review of your estate assets, there is no way to know whether the cheap document will accomplish its goals.

I once had a potential client say, "Why is a will so expensive if it's just a piece of paper that says who gets your stuff when you die?" My response: "It is just a document and a scalpel is just a knife, but in the hands of a professional it can save your life." Considering that your estate plan passes on your assets and values that it took a lifetime to accumulate, a wise steward should choose to work with an experienced local estate planning attorney during the planning process. Furthermore, an attorney with a Christian Worldview will be better equipped to counsel you regarding the complex legal and family issues surrounding your plan.

FYI: The Christian Legal Society's website is a great place to look for a Christian attorney in your jurisdiction (**www.clsnet.org/**).

CHAPTER 3

HEALTH CARE PLANNING AND HEALTH CARE DIRECTIVES

When wealth is lost, nothing is lost; when health is lost, something is lost; when character is lost, all is lost.
Billy Graham

But if anyone does not provide for his relatives, and especially for members of his household, he has denied the faith and is worse than an unbeliever.
1 Timothy 5:8

Stand up in the presence of the aged, show respect for the elderly and revere your God. I am the LORD.
Leviticus 19:32

"Honor your father and mother" (this is the first commandment with a promise), "that it may go well with you and that you may live long in the land."
Ephesians 6:2-3

Health Care Planning

The Andersons: A Case Study

As John and Beth Anderson sat in the waiting room at the downtown law firm of Braxton & Schultz, John began to remember back to a time in his life when things were simpler. A time when he and Beth were young parents and their two children, Amy and Matt were running around playfully in their back yard. John and Beth were never rich, but they had always been diligent about saving money and staying out of debt. Even with an average income, through the years they were able to build up a nest egg so that they could retire and eventfully pass on their possessions to their children. Like many other people in their late seventies, the Anderson's were worried that nursing home care in their later years could eat up their estate and leave their children with nothing.

Anxious to meet the attorney, John looked to his left seeking reassurance from his wife of 51 years. Sensing his anxiety, Beth lovingly squeezed his hand as if to say it was all going to work out. John then looked to his right to find reassuring smiles from both Amy and Matt. "This guy is really good dad, you don't have anything to worry about," explained Matt. Upon Matt's request, John had reluctantly agreed to meet elder law attorney Don Braxton to discuss he and his wife's strategy for nursing home care and estate planning. Don was a golfing buddy of Matt's and most of Matt's friends at the country club had worked with Don to prepare their estate plan. Neither John nor Beth liked the idea of being in a nursing home, but between Matt and Amy's busy lives working and raising kids with their spouses, they knew they did not want to be a burden to either of the children in their final years.

"Mr. and Mrs. Anderson, Mr. Braxton is ready to see you now," said the receptionist. As John walked down the long hallway full of mahogany and original artwork he was still not comfortable with this meeting. As they took a left into the attorney's office, John was warmly greeted by Mr. Braxton, a sharply dressed middle-aged man with a friendly smile. After exchanging pleasantries, Mr. Braxton began talking to the Anderson's about the dangers of losing everything to pay for nursing home costs. He explained various estate planning and elder planning strategies that would be the silver bullet to take away the Anderson's fears and make sure that their estate was preserved. One such strategy included putting virtually everything they own into a trust and giving assets to their children so that they would eventually qualify for the state/federal medical insurance program for the needy, known as Medicaid. "In my opinion, that's really the only good option that you have," explained Mr. Braxton.

John sat up on the end of his chair and said, "So basically, my wife and I would take everything we have and put it into someone else's hands so that we wouldn't really own anything anymore?" "Yes, Mr. Anderson, that is the basic idea. After all, you have worked too hard to just give everything away to a nursing home and plus, you wouldn't want to be a burden on your kids later on. I mean, nobody really wants to be a burden. Besides, Matt and Amy have very busy lives and they won't have the time to look after you the way that you would need in your later years. The way I see it, this I the best solution for everybody." John sat back in the leather chair and thought to himself, "I certainly don't want us to be a burden on the kids, so maybe they are right; maybe this is the only option we have."

The Biblical Mandate to Care for Our Family

Unfortunately, the scenario above is far too common today. Driven by elderly couples' common fears that they will lose everything to nursing and medical care, Elder law has become an increasingly popular practice area for attorneys nationwide. Although there are some reputable planners in this area of the law, Elder law is often times wrought with abuse. To understand this concept, you must first understand the purpose behind the Medicaid system. Medicaid is the government insurance program that provides health care for the needy. Medicaid is a federal health care program, funded by both the federal and state government, which provides care for people and families with extremely low incomes and resources.

In other words, the program is designed to assist only the poverty stricken among us. In order to qualify, your monthly income must be less than $2,022 and additional assets (excluding your homestead and car) must be less than $2,000. Elder law planners assist clients with creating trusts that help them shield assets from being counted against them so that they can qualify under these poverty guidelines. Sometimes this is legitimate planning that makes sense for the client. But in my opinion, most of the time it is not.

Most of this type of planning is driven by greed and deception. Greed on the part of the huckster attorneys (who receive a hefty sum for the planning), the client (who does not want to spend their own money on long term health care), and often times the client's children (who want to make sure mom and dad don't spend all of "their" inheritance on nursing home costs). I can't tell you how many phone calls I have received over the years from folks wanting me to help them shield assets so that they can keep the nursing home from taking everything from them.

Almost every time, the person on the other end of the phone has an estate over $1 million. Conceptually, this means that the potential client, who can clearly afford to pay for their own health care, wants me to help them voluntarily impoverish themselves so that they can qualify for Medicaid. Not only is this deceptive (morally), it's pretty stupid to give up control of nearly all of your financial assets during your retirement years. Not to mention, someone has to pay for the healthcare costs of this client. Guess who that might be? The good old tax paying citizens of your state. This should not surprise me, because we live in a country where so many people believe that they are entitled to certain benefits in life and that someone else should have to pay for them. Unfortunately, "Elder Law" is fueled by the bankrupt notion that we are not financially responsible for our own or our family's health and well-being.

There are also a couple of dirty little secrets that most people don't realize about transferring your assets to qualify for Medicaid. First, assets that are transferred out of the clients name in order to qualify under the poverty guidelines are subject to a five (5) year eligibility look-back period. This means that even if a person reduces their income and assets below the eligibility guidelines, if care is needed within 5 years there is an eligibility penalty period based upon the amount of the gift. This means that someone could technically qualify for Medicaid but be penalized from receiving its benefits for a certain period of time at the moment that their health care needs are most critical.

Secondly, after the insured has passed away, the state government is required by federal and state law to seek recovery from the estate of the patient for any funds expended by Medicaid, up to the total amount paid by Medicaid. In other words, Medicaid gets their money back from the decedent's estate assets.

So what does this all mean for Christian families faced with potential nursing home and long term health care expenses? First, I believe that Christian children should honor their aging parents by taking care of them instead of looking for the first opportunity to put them in an assisted living facility so that they don't cramp their lifestyle. That may not be a popular idea in 21st century America, but it is a time tested biblical concept. Although I do recognize that there are circumstances where nursing home care may be the only legitimate option.

Secondly, people who can afford to pay for their own long-term health care, either through personal finances or long term care insurance, should pay their own way. Looking for deceptive "legal" loopholes so that someone else fits the bill does not honor God and it is not loving to our neighbors (those who really need Medicaid nor those who are left to pay for it). Not to mention it is a form of stealing, which God's law strictly forbids (Exodus 20:15).

Thirdly, the Medicaid system should be reserved for only the extremely poor among us. A philosophical argument on the necessity of Medicaid or the responsibility of government to provide health care for the poor is beyond the scope of this book. My point is that most people under the current system don't need Medicaid and often times middle class and upper middle class folks are the ones trying to qualify for it.

Jesus' Command to Take Care of Family

In Mark 7:1-13, a bunch of Pharisees and Scribes (lawyers) watched as Jesus' disciples ate food before engaging in the Jewish ceremonial washing of their hands. The group of lawyers (I am imagining a local bar function) ask Jesus, "Why do your disciples not walk according to the tradition of the elders, but eat with defiled hands?" Jesus replied, "You leave the commandment of God and hold to the tradition of men." He continues, "For Moses said, 'Honor your father and your mother'; and, 'Whoever reviles father or mother must surely die.' But you say, 'If a man tells his father or his mother, 'Whatever you would have gained from me is Corban' (that is, given to God) then you no longer permit him to do anything for his father or mother, thus making void the word of God by your tradition that you have handed down. And many such things you do."

In this scenario, Christ is describing a man whose parents are in need, but their son cannot help them financially because according to tradition, the subject property is Corban. Corban was a gift offered to God which was kept in the sacred treasury. Think of it as a sacred savings account. In this traditional practice, the son could set apart his savings and claim that it is devoted to God as Corban and therefore, unavailable to help his parents. This allowed the son to shirk his responsibility to honor his father and mother in an ultra-religious sort of way. The Pharisees and Scribes would encourage such a decision. However, Jesus said such a practice makes the word of God void.

We have modern day Corban accounts as well. Although they are typically called balanced portfolios, retirement accounts, savings accounts, ski-boats, second homes, and country club memberships. We use them to invest in the fleeting American Dream. The possessions themselves are not evil, however, if they are keeping us from following the biblical mandate to care for our aging parents during their golden years, we are making the word of God void.

PLANNING POINT

Purchasing a Long Term Care Insurance policy can make good financial sense in the right circumstances. This type of insurance typically pays for nursing care, assisted living, and home care. Although the monthly premiums can be quite expensive (depending on the type of coverage and the insured's health), paying for long-term health care out of pocket can have devastating effects on a family's financial portfolio. For example, the average private nursing home room for one year can cost around $90,000. Couples over the age of 55 should discuss this option with their financial advisor, preferably someone with a Christian Worldview who has been trained as a Kingdom Advisor. A financial advisor can also help you determine whether investing the monthly premiums in other investment vehicles in order to build your net worth might be a better option. An interesting development in this field is the use of hybrid life insurance policies with a long-term care rider. This financial tool can provide long term care coverage along with a life insurance death benefit for your family. This is a topic that most readers should discuss with their financial advisor.

Health Care Directives

The Jacobs Family: A Case Study

As the clock strikes 12, Adam realizes that it has been almost exactly three weeks since the accident. According to the police report, at 12:01 on a Tuesday, his father, Steve Jacob's, swerved to avoid a child running into the street after a soccer ball. Thankfully, Steve missed the child, but his car clipped the front end of an oncoming car. Fortunately, the other driver left the scene with only minor injuries, but Steve was rushed to the hospital with a head injury that had left him in a comma. At first, the doctors were optimistic about Steve's recovery, but as the days turned into weeks, the optimism faded with each new test result. The term "permanent vegetative state" was now being used to describe Steve's long-term outlook. The day before, Steve's neurologist told Adam and his two sisters, Julie and Brenda, that removing their father from life support might be in everyone's best interest.

This was a tough blow for the Jacob's family. Just 2 years ago they had lost their mother, Cathy, to cancer. Throughout that difficult time, they watched their father's faith never waiver as he trusted in God's plan for his and his wife's life. A veteran of Vietnam and a pastor for 40 years, Steve was always the spiritual and emotional rock of the family. In times like these, Adam and his sisters would normally seek their dad's wisdom, but now that was not possible.

Unfortunately, Steve did not have a health care power of attorney or a living will in place that would give his family direction in such a circumstance. Because no one had the legal authority to make medical decisions for Steve, Adam had to hire an attorney and pay several thousand dollars in order to be appointed as Steve's legal guardian through an emergency guardianship proceeding. As he looks down at his ailing father, Adam is faced with the impossible choice to keep him alive and hope for a miracle or follow the doctor's advice.

Close to Home

If you are like me, this story hits close to home. Many of us have been in a similar situation with a member of our own family. It can be agonizing for family members to make medical decisions for a loved one when there is not clear direction left by the incapacitated patient. The legal issues surrounding end of life planning are often ignored until it is too late. Being a wise steward of the gifts God has entrusted us should certainly include a strategy for medical incapacity.

PLANNING POINT

Many Americans learned about the importance of Health Care directives by watching the Terry Schiavo case unfold on the national news in 2005. Schiavo suffered severe brain damage during a cardiac arrest in her home in 1990. Her doctors diagnosed her as being in a persistent vegetative state. Since she did not have a living will or other health care directive in place which stated her wishes, in 1998, her husband Michael petitioned the Sixth Circuit Court of Florida to remove her feeding tube. Terry's parents fought against the feeding tube removal and a 7-year legal battle ensued. Ultimately, the appeals court upheld the original decision to remove the feeding tube and Schiavo died on March 31, 2005 amid national controversy.

End of Life Planning

Issues regarding end of life medical care can be extremely complex and even uncomfortable to address. But, planning for the unexpected can be critical for both you and your loved ones. As long as you are competent, you have the power to make your own health care decisions. However, if you are not able to speak for yourself due to injury or illness, someone will have to make those decisions for you. Health Care Directives allow you to name trusted persons to make medical decisions on your behalf if the need arises. Such persons are called your "Attorney-in-Fact" or "Agent." Without a Health Care Directive in place, the courts will have to name someone to make medical decisions for you. Therefore, Health Care Directives should be included in every person's estate planning and life planning portfolio. Health Care Directives come in a few different shapes and sizes. A review of the commonly used Health Care Directives below, will help you figure out which type of document is best for you.

Health Care Power of Attorney

A document which names someone to make health care decisions for you (your "attorney-in-fact") if you develop a condition or sustain an injury that makes it impossible for you to speak for yourself. This document gives your attorney-in-fact and doctor clear written instructions regarding the type of medical treatment you would want to receive in particular situations.

Living Will

A living will (not to be confused with a Last Will and Testament) is a document which directs your physician to either provide or withhold life sustaining medical care, such as nutrition and hydration, if you are terminally ill or unconscious. In many states, the Living Will is often combined with a Health Care Power of Attorney.

Will to Live

A "Will to Live" Power of Attorney is a pro life legal document which combines the Living Will and Health Care Power of Attorney into one document. The Will to Live Power of Attorney presumes that nutrition and hydration are necessary to sustain life, while at the same time giving the client the freedom to refuse medical treatment that may actually prolong their death. The Will to Live and similar pro-life documents are encouraged by such groups as the National Right to Life, various Catholic ministries, The Texas Right to Life (a Catholic organization) and the Evangelical Christian organization Focus on the Family.

Which Document Is Best for Me?

Choosing the appropriate health care documents should include careful reflection with the assistance of a physician, pastor, and family members. Personally, I have chosen the Will to Live provided by the National Right to Life. However, I don't pretend to have all of the answer's when it comes to end of life medical issues. I also understand that reasonable minds can differ on the specifics surrounding such ethical dilemmas. But, if I am going to err one way or the other on issues of life and death, I am going to err on the side of life. That is exactly what the Will to Live document does.

The document presumes that the patient wants to live unless there are specific instructions to the contrary. In Ecclesiastes 3:2, Solomon reminds us there is, "a time to be born, and a time to die." We also know from Job 1:21 that the Lord gives and takes away. The ultimate decision of life and death is in the Lord's hands. But I do believe that we honor God with our health care documents when we first seek direction in His word and also seek wise biblical counsel on the subject. Also, you never know when God might work a modern day miracle as we see in the stories below.

PLANNING POINT

Having Health Care Directives is critically important to your estate plan and your life plan. Everyone should have these documents in place. Please be proactive about this. Please do not put this off until a later time. The best time to execute the appropriate health care directives is now, when you don't need them.

Modern Day Miracles

Whether the Lord chooses to heal someone or allows them to die is up to Him and not us. Our ways are not His ways and our thoughts are not His thoughts. But there are times when he does choose to heal and miracles do still happen. Take Sam Schmid for example. An abcnews.com story from December 22, 2011, entitled Poised to Donate Organs, 21-Year Old Emerges From Coma, tells his remarkable story.

Sam, a business major at the University of Arizona, was critically injured in a car accident that left him brain dead. Tragically, Schmid's roommate and another friend were killed in the accident. Schmid was immediately rushed into surgery where specialists operated on an aneurism in his brain. For several days after the surgery Schmid did not respond and doctors discussed the possibility of taking him off of life support. His mother, Susan Regan said, "at some point, I knew we had to make some sort of decision, and I kept praying."

As doctors approached the subject of removing life support with his parents, Schmid started using his hands to respond to questions. A few days later, his doctors agreed that he would be able to fully recover from his injuries. His mother is certainly convinced that miracles still happen. Regan explained, "I tell everyone, if they want to call it a modern day miracle, this is a miracle. I have friends who are atheists who have called me and said, 'I am going back to church.' " Schmid's doctor said, "I am dumbfounded with his incredible recovery in such a short time. His recovery was really remarkable considering the extent of his lethal injuries."

Jill Finley also knows a thing or two about miracles. According to an msnbc.com article from September 10, 2007 entitled Doctors Pull Plug, Comatose Woman Wakes Up, Finley inexplicably survived a near death experience. One morning, Jill's husband Ryan found her unresponsive. He immediately began CPR and called 911. When the paramedics arrived they shocked her heart back to life and rushed her to the hospital where she was hooked up to a respirator. However, Jill was in a deep coma and unable to respond. Her outlook was bleak, but Ryan remained with her and would read the Bible to her as he lay in the bed next to his wife.

After a couple of weeks with no change, Ryan made the agonizing decision to remove his wife from life support. At 6pm on June 9th, 2007, Jill's doctors disconnected her from the life sustaining machines. About 11:45pm Jill said, "Get me out of here" and asked her husband to take her to her favorite Mexican restaurant. In an interview with NBC's Meredith Vieira, Finley described her experience by saying, "It's crazy. It's absolutely crazy. It is truly a miracle that I'm here talking to you today."

The Will to Live

As Christians, we know that all people are destined to die once (Hebrews 9:27). But none of us knows when our Lord will call us home to be in His presence. However, we do know that our lives on earth are to be used to bring glory and honor to His name. Again, God's ways are a mystery and I have personally witnessed Him stretching out His hand to both heal and call one of His Saints home. I just want to make sure in my life, I give Him room to work miracles and then trust in His timing. Regarding end of life medical decisions I believe the Will to Live document does just that. I don't have all of the theological and medical answers when it comes to this topic, but neither does anyone else. So, if I am going to err, I will err on the side of life and leave my destiny in my Creator's hands.

If you are interested in exploring the Will to Live concept a little more, I would recommend the following websites:

1. **www.nrlc.org/euthanasia/willtolive/index.html**
   (National Right to Life Website)
2. **www.all.org/article.php?id=10689**
   (American Life League- a Catholic pro-life organization)
3. **www.all.org/article.php?id=10686**
   (American Life League)
4. **www.family.org/socialissues/A000000371.cfm**
   (Focus on the Family Ministry).

CHAPTER 4

GREAT COMMISSION ESTATE AND GIFT PLANNING

Go therefore and make disciples of all nations, baptizing them in the name of the Father and of the Son and of the Holy Spirit, teaching them to observe all that I have commanded you. And behold, I am with you always, to the end of the age.
Matthew 28:19-20

As for the rich in this present age, charge them not to be haughty, nor to set their hopes on the uncertainty of riches, but on God, who richly provides us with everything to enjoy. They are to do good, to be rich in good works, to be generous and ready to share, thus storing up treasure for themselves as a good foundation for the future, so that they may take hold of that which is truly life.
1 Timothy 6:17-19

He has made everything beautiful in its time. He has also set eternity in the hearts of men; yet they cannot fathom what God has done from beginning to end.
Ecclesiastes 3:11

We make a living by what we get, but we make a life by what we give.
Sir Winston Churchill

If I had not tithed the first dollar I made I would not have tithed the first million dollars I made. Tell your readers to train the children to tithe, and they will grow up to be faithful stewards of the Lord.

John D. Rockefeller
American Entrepreneur & Philanthropist

Two common mistakes in churches today: prosperity theology (rich = godly) & poverty theology (poor = godly). The wise alternative = stewardship.

Mark Driscoll
Former Pastor of Mars Hill Church, Seattle, WA

Go change the world.

Jon Dupin
Pastor of Brentwood Church, Lynchburg, VA

Go Change the World

When I was in law school, my wife and I attended Brentwood Church in Lynchburg, VA. Our pastor, Jon Dupin, would end every sermon with the words "Go change the world." Man, I loved that. After a great sermon of learning God's truth he would end it with a plea to take action. Instead of simply letting the sermon change us individually, we were reminded each week that the Gospel of Jesus Christ is not meant for selfish consumption. It is meant to be shared. It is meant to make an impact in the world around us and in Jon's words, "bring a little more of heaven here on earth." That is the Great Commission that we see from Jesus Christ in Matthew 28 when he is physically about to leave this world to be with his Father- go change the world.

When I leave this life, I hope that my last wishes reflect my desire for change in this world. In Ecclesiastes, Solomon reminds us that God has put eternity in all of our hearts. In other words, our lives were meant to last beyond the grave. What we do in life makes a difference for eternity, either for good or for bad; either for God's Kingdom or for the enemy's agenda. I think the same can be said for our estate planning. With the right perspective I believe our estate plans can make a difference and help fulfill the Great Commission even after we have left this world to be with our Father. I like to call this Great Commission Estate Planning.

Consider this. Nearly half of the people in the world live on less than $2 per day and 80% live on less than $10 per day. About 30,000 children die of starvation every day. There are over 1.4 million children that die each year from lack of access to safe drinking water and sanitation. There are over 500 million orphaned children in the world. Almost 2 billion (1/3 of the world population) people have never heard the Gospel of Jesus Christ. Over 7,000 people groups are considered unreached and have never heard the Gospel. A little closer to home, there are nearly 700,000 homeless persons in America and nearly 50 million people live in poverty.

Using our estate plans as a tool, we can make a difference in the lives of people around the world by helping meet their physical and spiritual needs. And a charitable donation in our estate plan is perhaps the best opportunity we have to make a sizable gift to a church and/or Christian ministry considering that 1) there is money that is readily available and 2) we don't need it anymore because we are not here.

Great Commission Estate Planning in Action

I wanted to find out for myself what kind of an impact that Great Commission Estate Planning could have on the spiritually broken and needy throughout the world. To find some answers I needed to speak with folks whose ministries have boots on the ground. People that are changing lives. Universities that are training the next generation of world changers. And ministries that are reaching the poor, oppressed, and marginalized with the Gospel of Jesus. So I contacted a few very well respected Christian ministries and universities to hear their perspective. I had the privilege of interviewing Steve Nickel, J.D., Senior Gift Planning Counsel for Samaritan's Purse International Ministry; Jeff Rudder, Executive Director of the Young Life Foundation; Harold Knowles, Planned Giving Advisor for Liberty University; Vickie Butler, Senior Gift Officer, Susie Trentham, Advancement Services Director, Carson-Newman University; and Michael Occhipinti, Gift Planning Advisor for Wycliffe Bible

Translators. I am thankful to all of these ministries for their time and input. I hope that you, the reader, find their viewpoints to be both challenging and informative.

SAMARITAN'S PURSE

Interview with Steve Nickel, J.D.
Senior Gift Planning Counsel

Samaritan's Purse is an international Christian relief organization based in Boone, NC. Samaritan's Purse follows the example of the Good Samaritan by going to the aid of the world's poor, sick and suffering. For over 40 years Samaritan's Purse has been reaching hurting people in countries around the world with food, medicine, and other assistance in the name of Jesus Christ. Their work allows them to earn a hearing for the Gospel, and provides a platform for the Good News of eternal life through Jesus Christ to be preached to lost souls.

Their emergency relief programs provide assistance to the victims of natural disaster, war, disease, and famine. Their vocational programs help impoverished people break the cycle of poverty. And their medical projects provide first class treatment in the name of the Great Physician. According to their mission statement, Samaritan's Purse is a "nondenominational evangelical Christian organization providing spiritual and physical aid to hurting people around the world." The organization is led by its President and CEO Franklin Graham, the son of evangelist Billy Graham.

Steve Nickel is an attorney on staff with Samaritan's Purse who is responsible for providing gift planning counsel to the ministry's donors. As I discussed the impact of planned giving on their ministry, I was surprised to hear that most of the gifts they receive are small contributions. Whether gifts of cash, stocks, or real estate during lifetime or bequests through a Will, their global ministry is largely supported by generous gifts from people with modest estates. Everyday people with ordinary means are making an impact for the Gospel. Often, these gifts come from people who are willing to give back to God through their Will.

According to Steve, the estate gifts the ministry receives are on average 7 times greater than the lifetime gifts from the same donors. After acknowledging that many Christians don't consider giving to the Lord from their estate, Steve explained, "10% of what I leave behind is a reasonable service of worship to God for what he has provided and it sets an example for children and grandchildren. Giving is at the heart of who God is and if we want to be like God, we are to be givers." He continued, "Doesn't God give the ability to create wealth and isn't He honored when we acknowledge Him by giving to Him out of our increase?"

Then Steve shared his financial planning wheel with me (see Figure 4.1 below). This is an illustration that he uses with the ministry's donors to help them understand the centrality of Christ in our financial lives. At the center of the wheel is Christ. At the end of each spoke are the essential components of financial planning and estate planning which include Current Needs, Asset Management, Future Needs, Tax Planning, Family Legacy, and Eternal Legacy (this book primarily deals with the Eternal Legacy component).

Steve said, "You can't become obsessed with particular items of a financial plan or the wheel will be out of balance. The center must be Christ because He never changes, and if we center Him among our financial priorities, then the wheel is able to move smoothly." He then explained how he was able to counsel a business owner and potential donor in Kentucky by using this model. The gentleman was not a believer at the time and their conversation opened the door for Steve to lead him to faith in Christ. By keeping Christ at the center of the planned giving conversation, God used Steve to change a man's life forever. That too should be the goal of every Christian in the process of planning their estate. Keep Christ at the center and use your resources to change lives eternally.

www.samaritanspurse.org

Figure 4.1
Christ-Centered Financial Planning Wheel

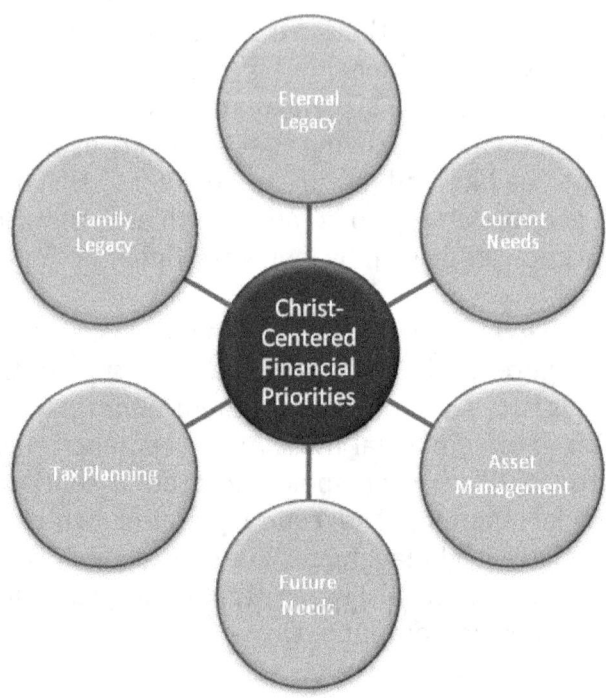

Used with the permission of Samaritan's Purse

YOUNG LIFE

Interview with Jeff Rudder
Executive Director, The Young Life Foundation

In 1939, Jim Rayburn, a young Presbyterian youth leader and seminary student in Gainesville, Texas, was given a challenge. A local minister invited him to consider the neighborhood high school as his parish and develop ways of contacting kids who had no interest in church. Rayburn started a weekly "club" for kids. There was singing, a skit or two and a simple message about Jesus Christ. Club attendance increased dramatically when they started meeting in the homes of the young people.

After graduating from seminary, Rayburn and four other seminarians collaborated, and Young Life was officially born on Oct. 16, 1941, with its own board of trustees. They developed the club idea throughout Texas, with an emphasis on showing kids that faith in God can be not only fun, but exhilarating and life-changing. Today Young Life continues to press toward the goal of reaching two million kids a year through their *Reaching a World of Kids* initiative. To do this, they are looking to mobilize more than 80,000 volunteers and establish 8,000 ministry locations. They are uniquely positioned and prepared to respond to this opportunity by doing what they do best for more kids in more places. They will do this through sustaining and starting ministries, leveraging the power of their volunteers and expanding their camping programs. Young Life's mission remains the same — to introduce adolescents to Jesus Christ and to help them grow in their faith. This happens when caring adults build genuine friendships and earn the right to be heard with their young friends. For more than seven decades, God has blessed Young Life, increasing its staff numbers from five to more than 3,500 — from one club in Texas to clubs in nearly every corner of the world. Young Life is now headquartered in Colorado Springs, Colorado.

I had the privilege of interviewing Jeff Rudder, the Executive Director of the Young Life Foundation, about the impact that giving has on this ministry. Jeff explained that Young Life is now reaching kids for Christ in over 90 countries. According to Jeff, Young Life works to build non-judgmental relationships with kids. They earn the right to be heard with unreached kids, and point to the truth about Jesus when the right opportunity presents itself. The fruit of the harvest is often seen when teens spend a week at one of Young Life's many camps throughout the U.S. I have personally spent a week at Frontier Ranch in Buena Vista, Colorado.

For most of the campers, their lives are never the same after that experience. Many of them decide to follow Christ, and of course, that changes the entire direction of their life. Jeff mentioned that many campers need financial assistance to get to camp. In other words, without individual donors helping the ministry financially, fewer campers have the opportunity to be introduced to the Savior. Surprisingly, out of the ministry's annual budget of $260 million, only about $2 million comes from estate gifts. Most of the gifts come from the lifetime giving of individual donors. In Jeff's words, "$50 or $100 a month givers are the driving force behind our yearly budget."

In fact, Jeff was really excited about something called the Campership Legacy Fund. This is a fund that has been set up in order 1) to help kids go to camp now, while the donor is alive to appreciate the impact of their gifts, and 2) help encourage donors to use estate gifts to build a pipeline for kids to go to camp in the future. As of the printing of this book, over 140 donors had pledged future gifts of $55 million to the Campership Legacy Fund. Jeff also outlined the six promises that Young Life makes to its donors through the Campership Legacy Fund:

1. Strategic: we are going to reach unreached kids with the message of Jesus.
2. Intentional: the local staff sends a written application to the headquarters requesting financial assistance to allow unreached kids to go to camp.
3. Generous: the Foundation pays out 10% per year from the fund, regardless of market performance. "In God we trust," is the way that Jeff put it.
4. Family Legacy: twice a year Young Life produces reports to donors about fund performance and includes stories of kids coming to Christ at Camp. This is their way of putting a stake in the ground to share their belief system across generations

5. Transparency: Young Life employs outside investment counsel and periodic financial reports are provided to its donors.
6. Camp Connected: donors are invited to "come and see" what they are investing in by coming to camp to see how their gift is making an impact on camper's lives.

I concluded my interview with Jeff by asking him to tell me a story of how radical generosity had impacted the ministry of Young Life. Frankly, I was overwhelmed by his response. In the 1980's there was a piece of real estate in Oregon owned by a cult, whose members actually tried to kill a U.S. Attorney. A generous family purchased this property and gave it to Young Life. The cult had already put in some infrastructure such as roads, water, and electricity, so the property was already primed to be improved into a youth camp. Today, there are 10,000 kids who come to this camp every year to hear the Gospel of Jesus. This property that was meant for harm by Satan, has been redeemed for God's kingdom, thanks to the radically generous hearts of one family.

www.younglife.org

WYCLIFFE BIBLE TRANSLATORS

Interview with Michael Occhipinti
Gift Planning Advisor

Wycliffe was founded in 1942 by William Cameron Townsend. A missionary to the Cakchiquel Indians of Guatemala, Townsend caught the vision for translation after Cakchiquel-speaking men expressed their concern and surprise that God did not speak their language.

Townsend resolved that every man, woman and child should be able to read God's Word in their own language. Borrowing the name of the Reformation hero, **John Wycliffe**, who first translated the Bible into English, Townsend founded Camp

Wycliffe in 1934 as a linguistics training school. By 1942, Camp Wycliffe had grown into two affiliate organizations, Wycliffe Bible Translators and the **Summer Institute of Linguistics (SIL)**.

Today, SIL and Wycliffe Bible Translators work together to translate Scripture, train field personnel and promote interest in translation. **More than 700** translations have been completed, and hundreds more are in the process. With God's provision, Townsend's vision will be realized.

Michael Occhipinti is a Gift Planning Advisor for Wycliffe who is responsible for advising donors in the Western region of the United States. Over a plate of pancakes, Michael shared his insights regarding the role that planned giving has in providing Bible translations to the 180 million people in the world that do not have scripture in their own language. Like many of the other ministries I talked to, estate giving was certainly important to Wycliffe's mission, providing several million dollars annually. According to Michael, "These gifts combined with current dollars are our lifeblood, allowing Wycliffe missionaries to continue their task of translating the Bible into the over 1,900 languages that still need translation." He continued, "The gifts we receive can be as little as a few dollars or as great as $1 million and everything in between. From the widow's mite to Solomon's gifts."

Regarding estate gifts, he remarked, "Do you really think your kids are going to miss 10% of your estate? How much is enough for your kids? A lot of people have not asked that question. Who owns it? Have you really talked to God about what you should do with His money? A lot of times people are locked into tradition when it comes to estate planning, but they are missing the point. It's the difference between a temporal and eternal perspective on money. A final gift from your estate to ministries that you have supported during your lifetime allows you to share that eternal perspective with your children and grandchildren."

Wycliffe has a God sized goal to see a Bible translation program in progress in every language still needing one by 2025. For more information on their work around the world please visit their website: **www.wycliffe.org**

CARSON-NEWMAN UNIVERSITY

Interview with Vickie Butler, Senior Gift Officer
Susie Trentham, Advancement Services Director

Carson-Newman University is a Christian liberal arts college located in Jefferson City, Tennessee. Carson-Newman has over 2,300 students in 90 different academic programs. It was recently named as a Best College in the Southeast by The Princeton Review and America's #2 ranked college for community service by Washington Monthly. Carson-Newman's mission as Christian educators is to help students reach their full potential as educated citizens and worldwide servant-leaders.

According to Vickie Butler, like many other Christian universities in America, the mission of Carson-Newman is realized because of lifetime gifts, estate plan gifts, and charitable gift annuities from generous donors. In fact, Susie Trentham estimated that about 25% of the university's annual revenues come from lifetime gifts. Butler explained, "Any format of donor support enhances our ministry and mission. Planned giving allows flexibility for financial gifts which might otherwise not be possible for the donor." Just like most of the other ministries or universities I interviewed, Carson-Newman believes that there is, in fact, a gap between the number of lifetime donors they have and the number of estate gifts they receive from such donors.

Currently, Carson-Newman is embarking on a $25 million "Student First" scholarship campaign. During the announcement of the new campaign, Carson-Newman's President Randall O'Brien said, "Our students, under the Lord, are first. They are why we are here. Without them we would have no mission, no calling, no purpose for existence." Interestingly, country and bluegrass legend Ricky Skaggs has graciously participated in the campaign through the creation of the Ricky Skaggs Endowed Scholarship.

Carson-Newman recently received a $1 million outright gift to their scholarship endowment from a generous donor. This gift was truly part of a family legacy at the school as the donor made the gift in honor of his mother, a 1945 graduate. Fifteen years earlier, the donor's father had endowed the scholarship in honor of his wife, a woman who taught English to American immigrants. His son's gift continued the family's commitment to giving. In a beautiful description of his gift, the donor said, "My prayer is that this endowed scholarship fund in my mother's name, as founded by my father, will honor my parents and provide many generations of worthy students the same opportunity to receive the quality education from Carson-Newman that my family has enjoyed for more than 100 years." This gift was about much more than money; it was about the radical generosity and faithfulness of an entire family.

For more information about Carson-Newman University, visit: **www.cn.edu**.

LIBERTY UNIVERSITY

Interview with Harold Knowles
Senior Planned Giving Officer

Located in the Foothills of the Blue Ridge Mountains in Lynchburg, VA, Liberty University is the largest Christian university in the world. Liberty has over 15,000 on campus students and about 100,000 online students. In fact, Liberty is the nation's largest private university and the 7th largest four-year university. Since 1971, the mission of Liberty University has been to develop Christ-centered men and women with the values, knowledge, and skills essential for impacting tomorrow's world. With a unique heritage and an ever-expanding influence,

Liberty remains steadfast in its commitment of *Training Champions for Christ.*

I caught up with Harold Knowles, Liberty's Senior Planned Giving Officer for Estate Planning to discuss how generosity enables students to learn and share the gospel in the world. Harold has worked in the University's planned giving department for 36 years. During the time, he has seen how God has used gifts from generous donors to grow the university from a few students into the largest university in the state of Virginia. One way that has happened is through donations to scholarship funds for students. Once a scholarship fund has $50,000 in it, the income is then used to help a student attend Liberty. Many times the donor will even specify that the scholarship should go to persons from their hometown, region of the country, or perhaps from the field of study that the donor majored in.

Another charitable tool that donors to Liberty often utilize is the charitable gift annuity. This allows the donor to further the University's mission while receiving an income stream for life. Interestingly, one donor gave LU his airplane in exchange for a lifetime income. Upon his subsequent passing, his wife will continue to receive an income stream for her lifetime. According to Mr. Knowles, many donors choose gift annuities as part of their lifetime giving and also leave a bequest to the University in their Will. This allows the donor to maximize their income tax and estate tax savings, while making a lasting impact on the students training to be champions for Christ in their chosen profession.

Concerning estate bequests, Mr. Knowles explained, "Many of our donors believe that their kids will be better off financially and spiritually with 90% of the estate than they will be with 100% of the estate." He continued, "As a Christian, tithing through your estate plan is a win-win situation."

For more information about Liberty University planned giving, please visit: **www.lugiving.com**

Wyatt Wilson is Liberty's planned giving officer for the state of Colorado: **wwwilson@liberty.edu**

Estate Planning Generosity Gap

As I wrapped up my interviews with various ministries, I noticed that this same theme of consistent lifetime giving by donors followed by inconsistent estate plan giving kept coming up. Why do so many faithful Christian givers fail to make a "Kingdom Gift" from their estate plan? I think Michael Occhipinti shed some light on this when he said, "People are locked into tradition when it comes to estate planning. It is the difference between a temporal and eternal perspective."

Personally, I believe that many Christians are doing a great job of making Christ the center of their financial lives (see Figure 4.1 above on p. 114), but when it comes to the final distribution of our assets, we are following the tradition of leaving everything to our children. That is why I felt it was important to write this book. To make Christians aware of the opportunities they are missing out on to change the world and leave a financial and spiritual legacy to their children.

As I mentioned earlier, our estate plan is perhaps the best opportunity we have to make a sizable gift to a church and/or Christian ministry considering that 1) there is money that is readily available and 2) we don't need it anymore because we are not here. It is also our last opportunity to show our children that Christ should always remain in the center of all that we do, in this life and the next.

> **PLANNING POINT**
>
> In Acts 1:8, Jesus tells his followers that they will be his witnesses in Jerusalem, Judea, Samaria, and to the end of the earth. Using Acts 1:8 as a guide for Great Commission Estate Planning allows you to use your gifts to make an impact for Christ's Kingdom in your community and beyond. Designating a portion of your estate to your local church first, then to local ministries, then to global ministries allows your gift to sow seeds for a spiritual harvest throughout the world.

WAYS TO GIVE TO A CHURCH, UNIVERSITY, OR MINISTRY

Once you have decided to give, the next steps are to decide how to give, what to give, and how much to give. Below are some examples of the ways you can give to your church, favorite university, or other ministries. Although many of these topics are discussed in earlier chapters, a brief overview of the avenues for giving seemed appropriate to include in this chapter as well.

Gifts During Your Lifetime

Outright Gifts of Cash

With so many fancy estate planning and gift planning legal tools available, a simple gift of cash to a ministry or your church during your lifetime often gets overlooked. However, simple outright gifts can be vital to Christian ministries and it allows the donor to experience the joy of giving during their life. Not to mention, the donor often times can physically see how their gift impacts the mission of the organization. The donor also receives a charitable income tax deduction.

Gifts of Stocks & Bonds

A gift of your securities, including your stocks, mutual funds, or bonds, is an easy way for you to make a gift. By making a gift of your appreciated securities, you can avoid paying capital gains tax that would otherwise be due if you sold these assets. Additionally, you will receive a charitable income tax deduction.

Gifts of Real Estate

A gift of your real property (such as your home, vacation property, vacant land, farmland, ranch or commercial property) can make a great gift. If you own appreciated real property, you can avoid paying capital gains tax by gifting the property to your church or a ministry. Additionally, you will receive a charitable income tax deduction. The value of the gift is determined by a fair market value appraisal of the property.

Gift of Retirement Accounts

A gift of your retirement assets, such as a gift from your IRA, 401k, 403b, pension or other tax deferred plan, can be an excellent way to make a charitable gift. Prior to 2015, federal law allowed direct donations to charities from IRA's via IRA Charitable Rollovers. This allowed taxpayers over 70 ½ to make tax-free charitable gifts of up to $100,000 per year directly from their retirement accounts to eligible charities, including their favorite college or university.

However, as of the writing of this book, the IRA Charitable Rollover remains in limbo. The IRA Charitable Rollover expired on December 31, 2014. However, on February 12, 2015, the U.S. House of Representatives passed the America Gives More Act of 2015, which would make the IRA Charitable Rollover permanent. The fate of the bill now rests with the U.S. Senate, and President Obama has indicated that he will veto the bill if it reaches his desk. This could be a great lifetime giving tool, but the reader should be diligent to seek the advice of legal and tax counsel to get the latest tax law updates prior to making such gifts.

A great testamentary strategy (i.e., upon husband and wife's death) is to leave assets that can receive a stepped up tax basis (i.e., real estate or appreciated securities in a taxable account) or assets that have tax free income (i.e., Roth IRA) to the children and assets that are subject to income taxes (i.e., Traditional IRAs and 401(k)s) to charity. This results in an estate tax charitable deduction and income tax avoidance. Income taxes would be paid on such assets left to children, but the charity is able to use 100% of the assets to further their purposes.

Charitable Gift Annuity

A gift annuity is a contract between you and a charity (often a University) whereby you make a charitable gift to the charity and the charity agrees to pay you and/or your loved ones a fixed annuity payment for life. The size of the payment will be dependent on the size of the gift and the age of the donor at that time. A donor may also make a gift and defer the payments until a later time, which allows for a larger immediate income tax deduction and higher payouts once the payments begin.

Gift annuities are not insured by any government agency, but they are backed by the assets of the charity or University offering the gift annuity. For donors looking to turn current assets into a fixed income stream, while helping a favorite charity and receiving an immediate income tax deduction, a Charitable Gift Annuity may be a great vehicle to accomplish your goals. The planned giving page for Liberty University has some very helpful information on this topic: lugiving.com/?pageID=12

Gifts to Donor-Advised Funds

According to the Internal Revenue Service definition, a donor advised fund is a separately identified fund or account that is maintained and operated by a section 501(c)(3) nonprofit organization (i.e., public charity). Each account is composed of contributions made by individual donors. Once the donor makes the irrevocable contribution, the organization has legal control over it. However, the donor, or the donor's representative, retains advisory privileges with respect to the distribution of funds and the investment of assets in the account.

A DAF is a great charitable planning tool because 1) the donor receives an immediate income tax deduction for the charitable gift and 2) the donor can periodically recommend that the nonprofit provide grants to other nonprofit organizations of their choosing on their own timetable. Although the charity who manages the DAF owns the assets, the donor acts as an advisor over the funds and recommends grants to the charity.

When using a Christian charity, a believer is able to recommend grants to various ministries as they become aware of specific needs. It gives the donor the advantage of an income tax deduction coupled with the freedom to financially support ministries they are passionate about. An easy way to think about a donor-advised fund is like a charitable savings account: a donor contributes to the fund as frequently as they like and then recommends grants to their favorite charity when they are ready. In summary:

1. You make an irrevocable contribution of assets to a Nonprofit DAF.
2. You immediately receive the maximum income tax deduction that the IRS allows (50% of adjusted gross income; can be carried forward for up to 5 years).
3. You name your donor-advised fund account and advisors.
4. Your contribution is placed into a donor-advised fund account where it can be invested and grow tax free.
5. At any time afterward, you can recommend grants from your account to qualified charities.

Figure 4.2
Gifts to Donor Advised Fund

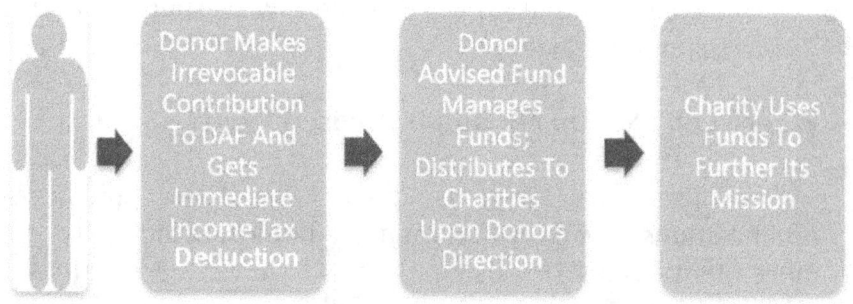

See Appendices H & I, Pages 169, 170 for more info.

Private Foundations

A private foundation is charitable nonprofit organization that is usually created through a single primary donation from an individual or a business, whose funds and programs are managed by its own trustees or directors. Rather than funding its ongoing operations through periodic donations, a private foundation generates income by investing its initial donation, often disbursing the bulk of its investment income each year to desired charitable activities. Private foundations are typically created by wealthy families who wish to create an organization that their family can control in order to achieve their philanthropic goals.

The IRS applies strict rules to Private Foundations, including:

1. Required to pay out to charity at least 5% of their asset value annually or be subject to penalty.
2. A 1% to 2% excise tax on investment income is imposed annually.
3. Penalties are imposed on transactions between the foundation and its donors or mangers. The foundation

cannot benefit a private individual.
4. Income tax deductions are limited to 20% (gifts of stock or real property) or 30% (gifts of cash) of adjusted gross income (compared to 30% and 50% respectively for gifts to public charities).

Where Can I Set Up My Donor Advised Fund?

There are several great Christian philanthropic organizations that offer donor advised funds. Although there are more that what is listed here, I have personally built relationships with people in the following organizations and I wholeheartedly endorse the work they are doing to advance God's Kingdom.

WaterStone

Since WaterStone was incorporated in 1980 as the Christian Community Foundation, their passion and expertise as business professionals have helped entrepreneurs, business executives, and intergenerational family business owners eliminate estate taxes, minimize capital gains, decrease annual income taxes and increase their ability to give to their favorite charities and ministries. Through strong leadership coupled with the hearts and actions of their donors, WaterStone has become a launching pad for Kingdom work nationally and internationally.

WaterStone is not about giving as usual. In fact, many people come to WaterStone exactly for that reason: they innovate. They have earned a reputation over the past 30 years of being able to transform any kind of asset into living water—a water that renews, heals, satisfies thirst and yields eternal life.

Their team will look strategically and holistically at your assets and be a trusted long-term partner to ensure your plans are executed even past your lifetime. With over 30 years of experience, WaterStone has distributed over $300 million of assets to support: housing and food for Ethiopian women, third-world orphanages, various projects for special needs children, HIV/AIDS programs in Africa, Nepalese churches, Zimbabwean schools, hurricane Katrina relief, refurbishment of C.S. Lewis' Oxford home, campus ministry, and medical mission trips. Their goal is to achieve $1 billion in giving by 2020.

http://waterstone.org

The Orchard Foundation

The Orchard Foundation is a fiduciary ministry which offers a wide range of gift planning tools to individuals, families, and ministry organizations who desire to make the most of their God-given resources to meet personal, family, and charitable objectives. The Orchard Foundation manages a variety of instruments that offer donors creative options for charitable giving. Since the 1960s, The Orchard Foundation has offered a unique blend of quality asset management combined with integrity, client-focused service, and excellence.

www.Inspire-Giving.com

National Christian Foundation

Founded by Ron Blue, Larry Burkett, and attorney Terry Parker, National Christian Foundation (NCF) is the largest Christian grant-making foundation in the world. Their innovative, tax-smart solutions help you simplify your giving, multiply your impact, and glorify God. Since 1982, they have received $6 billion in contributions and made over $5 billion in grants to thousands of churches, ministries, and nonprofits.

In an interview with Jeanne McMains, JD, Vice-President of Gift Planning for the National Christian foundation, I learned that NCF currently has over 17,000 family donor advised funds. Headquartered in Atlanta Georgia, NCF now has 30 offices throughout the U.S. including one in Littleton, Colorado. Jeanne encourages her clients to engage in "Impact Driven Estate

Design." The estate plan is not built primarily on tax planning or legal tools, but on the impact it will have in the world. In Jeanne's words, "It's dangerous to pass on wealth without wisdom." She continued, "Leave your kids with life shaping experience rather than just money without connection."

She recalled several clients who had practiced this type of planning. One client's Last Will gave $50,0000 to each grandchild who spends one year on the Christian mission field internationally. The grandchildren did not have to do it, but they were encouraged to. In the grandfather's mind, this would transform his grandchildren's ideas regarding wealth and resources.

Another client set up a common trust for his grandchildren that would pay for each of them to go to a Christian summer camp until they reached college. Upon entering college, the trust would pay for each grandchild to go on up to three short term overseas mission trips per year.

www.nationalchristian.com/home

Charitable Remainder Trust (CRT)

A Charitable Remainder Trust can be a highly effective financial and estate planning tool. This irrevocable trust provides an income stream to the donor or to other noncharitable beneficiaries for life or for a term of years and pays the remainder interest in the trust to one or more qualified charitable organizations. A CRT can be either inter vivos or testamentary in nature, but typically they are created inter vivos (during the donor's lifetime). An inter vivos CRT is created by a written irrevocable trust agreement executed by the donor and the trustee during the donor's lifetime. A testamentary CRT is created by the donors Will or Revocable Living Trust. An in-depth look at this tool can be found on p. 47 above.

Charitable Lead Trust (CLT)

A Charitable Lead Trust provides an income stream to one or more qualified charitable organizations for the life of a natural person or for a term of years and upon termination, distributes the remaining trust assets to the donor's non-charitable beneficiaries. A CLT is primarily used by individuals who wish to benefit a charity first, with the property ultimately passing to family members at reduced tax rates. A CLT is typically structured as an irrevocable trust during life, but it can also be created as a testamentary trust. An in-depth look at this tool can be found on p. 53 above.

Gifts Upon Your Death

Specific Bequests of Cash, Property, or Securities in Your Last Will or Revocable Living Trust

Specific Bequests in a Will or Revocable Living Trust are specified items that you want to pass to a particular person or charity. For example a cash bequest of $10,000 to your church is a specific bequest. So is a bequest of your car to one of your children. These items will be distributed to the specified individuals before any other estate property is distributed. The Residuary Estate is whatever is left over once all specific bequests have been made. A specific bequest of cash or a particular assets to church or ministry can be a great tool to leave a legacy to the ministry and reduce your taxable estate.

Residuary Bequests in Your Last Will or Revocable Living Trust

Every Last Will and Revocable Living Trust should have a Residuary Clause. This clause specifies where you want the remainder of your property to go once any specific bequests have been made. A typical residuary clause might read, "To my children who survive me, per capita at each generation." This would leave your residuary to your children equally. However, you can also add language to your Last Will or Revocable Living Trust, which will leave a percentage of your residuary to your church or favorite ministry. The percentages can be split up between family and charity depending on your wishes.

It is a good idea to contact the specific ministry which you wish to benefit to ask them for the specific language they would prefer your attorney to use. Listing a church or charity as a contingent beneficiary to receive the bequest of a child who predeceases you, is an option as well. Below is a sample residuary bequest of 20% to a chosen ministry.

Twenty Percent (20%) to Ravi Zacharias International Ministries, located at 4725 Peachtree Corners Circle, Suite 250, Norcross, GA 30092, for its unrestricted use and purpose.

Life Insurance Beneficiary

Term life insurance products have made it very easy to leverage a small monthly or yearly premium into a large death benefit payout for beneficiaries of the policy. This also presents a great opportunity to provide a significant gift to church or ministry who would be named as a beneficiary. The church or ministry might be listed as the sole beneficiary, or they may be listed as one of the beneficiaries. One interesting strategy I have seen is treating the church/ministry like one of the kids. For example, if a decedent has 3 children, then name the 3 children and the church/ministry as equal beneficiaries of the life insurance. That way, the children receive 25% each (75% collectively), and the church/ministry receives 25%. The decedent's estate will also receive an estate tax charitable deduction for the amount of the gift.

Generosity in Action

How Much Is Enough?

Recently, while waiting in a very long line at the post office, I noticed an article on the wall about a man named Winfield Scott Stratton. Stratton went from being a working class carpenter to a multi-millionaire entrepreneur and renowned philanthropist. Born in Indiana in 1848, Stratton left Indiana for Colorado Springs at the age of 24 to make his fortune in the West. He found a job as a carpenter, but he spent his summers prospecting for gold and silver throughout Colorado. On July 4, 1891 he staked a claim near Cripple Creek and found a "fabulously rich" vein of gold. In 1899, after digging $2 million from the mine, he sold it for $10 million.

Regarding his wealth, Stratton said, "Too much money is not good for any man. I have too much and it's not good for me. $100,000 is as much as the man of ordinary intelligence can take." Stratton helped build much of downtown Colorado Springs and donated generously to many charitable causes. Upon his death, the bulk of his estate went to establish a shelter for the poor in Colorado Springs.

Reading this story made me ask myself the question- how much is enough? I believe that when many Christians are considering charitable giving in their life plan and estate plan they start with the question- how much should I give? I address that question below, but I believe that is the second question we should be asking. The first question should be "how much is enough?" For Stratton it was $100,000 in the late 1800's. What should it be for you?

There is no formula here and everyone will likely have a different answer, but at some point there is a number that allows a person to follow the biblical mandate to take care of their family and anything beyond that is not necessary. In fact, anything beyond that are wasted assets that could be expanding

God's Kingdom. As you prayerfully ask yourself this critical question, remember the Parable of the Rich Fool.

> *Someone in the crowd said to him, "Teacher, tell my brother to divide the inheritance with me." But he said to him, "Man, who made me a judge or arbitrator over you?" And he said to them, "Take care, and be on your guard against all covetousness, for one's life does not consist in the abundance of his possessions." And he told them a parable, saying, "The land of a rich man produced plentifully, and he thought to himself, 'What shall I do, for I have nowhere to store my crops?' And he said, 'I will do this: I will tear down my barns and build larger ones, and there I will store all my grain and my goods. And I will say to my soul, "Soul, you have ample goods laid up for many years; relax, eat, drink, be merry."' But God said to him, 'Fool! This night your soul is required of you, and the things you have prepared, whose will they be?' So is the one who lays up treasure for himself and is not rich toward God."*
>
> Luke 12:13-21

A great read on the topic is a small book by Leo Tolstoy (forward by Christian author Os Guinness) called *How Much Land Does a Man Need?*

How Much Should I Give?

I recently read a Facebook post about stewardship by Mark Driscoll, former teaching pastor of Mars Hill Church in Seattle, Washington, that made a ton of sense.

> *Two common mistakes in churches today:*
> *Prosperity theology   (rich = godly)*
> *Poverty theology   (poor = godly)*
> *The wise alternative   = stewardship.*

I think this is spot on. The scriptures are full of stories of Godly men and women from various walks of life. Some were poor fishermen. Some were wealthy kings. Some peasant girls. Some queens. But the Lord used them all and their resources (or lack thereof) to bring Him glory. All of us have been blessed with differing levels of material blessings. However, the key to making an impact for the Kingdom is to steward your five loaves and two fish and trust Christ to multiply your giving.

The Generosity Matrix

As you consider how to be a steward of what God has entrusted to you, I would recommend taking a look at a blog post entitled *The Generosity Matrix*, by pastor J.D. Greear*.

www.jdgreear.com/my_weblog/2011/09/the-generosity-matrix.html

Greear explains that, "there seem to be 2 extremes when it comes to how Christians view their relationship with their possessions. Extreme #1: God wants 10%; after that you can do whatever you want with your money. Extreme #2: God's only intention for our money is that we give it away to the poor or for world evangelization. Thus, if there's something you could give away and still survive, you should give it away. Each of our luxuries is the blood of the poor."

He continues, "In contrast to both of these extremes, I think Scripture teaches us to view our possessions through a *matrix* (cue now your 'red pill'/'blue pill' imagery and a disturbing mental image of Laurence Fishburne with that gap in his teeth). What do I mean by matrix? A matrix is a set of principles we must hold in tension. We like rules, formulas, and black and white prescriptions. Instead, the Bible gives complementary values we should prize in our hearts. Individual decisions arise out of processing them through that matrix. When it comes to our money, I see 6 principles the Bible puts forward. *Any one of these principles, taken alone, will lead you out of balance.* But holding all 6 in reverent tension can provide you with a balanced approach to your money that allows you to be freely generous with your money and also to enjoy the things that God has put into your life." His six principles are as follows:

1. God gives excess to some so that they can share with those who have less.
2. Jesus' radical generosity toward us should be to us a model and motivation for radical generosity with others.
3. The Holy Spirit must guide us as to which sacrifices we are to make.
4. God delights in our enjoyment of His material gifts and gives us richly all things to enjoy.
5. We are not to trust in riches and not to define our lives by the abundance of our possessions.
6. Wealth building is wise.

So, how much should Christians give? We should give what we are compelled by the Sprit to give. We should give radically, because Jesus radically gave to us. Greear concludes, "...love for God and for others grows as we embrace the extravagant love of God for us. As we do that, your heart will change and you will give away money with radical generosity, freely, because you love God and His kingdom more than you love stuff, and you hold God as your security more than you find security in stuff. When our hearts have been quickened to understand and love the Gospel, our natural, un-coerced reaction will be to live sufficiently and give extravagantly."

* J.D. Greear is the lead pastor of Summit Church in Raleigh-Durham, NC. He is also the author of several books, including *Stop Asking Jesus Into Your Heart.*

Radical Generosity Stories

As Greear described above, Jesus' radical generosity toward us should be our model and motivation for radical generosity with others. This concept of radical generosity continued to come up as I was reading and researching for this book. Below are just a few examples of the inspirational stories I came across of people who were radically generous givers.

Robert G. LeTourneau

Born in 1888, Robert G. LeTourneau was known throughout the construction world as "The Dean of Earthmoving." At the age of 16 he gave his life to Christ and at the age of 30 he gave his business life to Christ as well. LeTourneau was an inventor of earthmoving equipment who secured over 300 patents during his lifetime. In fact, his machines represented nearly 70% of the earthmoving and equipment used during World War II. While the rest of the country was experiencing the Great Depression, LeTourneau's business became a multi-million dollar operation.

With the profits pouring in, his wife Evelyn suggested that they transition to a 90/10 split with the Lord. 90% went to the Lord and 10% went to RG and Evelyn. By 1959, after giving away over $10 million to ministry, their foundation was still worth $40 million. He and his wife established missionary ministries in Liberia, West Africa, Peru, and other South American countries. They also founded LeTourneau University in Longview, Texas. LeTourneau was also a leader in The Christian and Missionary Alliance. "The question," Le Tourneau said, "is not how much of my money I give to God, but rather how much of God's money I keep for myself."

Marvin & Helen Frey

Marvin and Helen Frey started a ministry in 1956 to serve street kids in New York City. Their ministry, the Children's Fund of New York, served at risk youth for 36 years through their city facilities and Christian camp in upstate New York. Upon Marvin's death, Helen sold the camp and used the proceeds to establish the Marvin and Helen Frey Scholarship Endowment. The endowment gives students on the lower east side of New York the opportunity to pursue Christian education or vocational training, opportunities that they would not otherwise have.

Over the past twelve years, seventeen scholarships have been awarded to students, including former gang members and orphans. At the age of 90, Helen is still involved with the scholarship endowment. Helen explains, "This endowment will perpetuate our life-long ministry of serving underprivileged youth. When I hear from recipients that they are the first in their family to go to college, and know that this endowment is the reason for that, I am overjoyed and I know Marvin would be too."

Used with the permission of The Orchard Foundation

James Cash Penney

A few years ago I was on a wild west fly fishing adventure with my good buddy and my dad. Our quest for trout took us to Kemmerer, Wyoming of all places. Although famous (in my mind) for having only one car dealership which only carries pickup trucks, Kemmerer is even more well know for its favorite son, James Cash (aka J.C.) Penney. Penney's first store, in Kemmerer in 1902, was called the Golden Rule Store and it was operated on the principle of treating customers the way you would want to be treated, a principle Penney's Baptist preacher father had taught him as a boy.

As one of America's leading businessmen heading into the Great Depression, Penney's business and personal life were spiraling out of control. With an estranged family and his business failing, he contemplated suicide. But, after checking into a sanitarium, he stumbled into the chapel and heard the scripture, "Come unto me all you that are heavy laden, and I will give you rest." At that moment this broken entrepreneur returned to the faith his parents had taught him when he was a child.

Penney described, "At that time something happened to me which I cannot explain. It was a life-changing miracle, and I've been a different person ever since. I saw God in his glory and planned to be baptized and to join a church. Suddenly needing to be heard, I cried inwardly, 'Lord, will you take care of me? I can do nothing for myself!' I felt I was passing out of darkness into light. In the midst of failure to believe, I was being helped back to believing." Until his death at 95, Penney gave millions of dollars to more than 100 organizations ministering in the United States and around the world. After his conversion, Penney often quoted his favorite Bible verse, "I have trusted in the Lord without wavering. Prove me, O Lord, and try me. Test my heart and my mind. For your steadfast love is before my eyes, and I will walk in faithfulness to you." (Psalms 26:1-2)

James Anderson

Despite his great wealth, James Anderson was known to take a bucket of water and clean up after surgical procedures in the third-world hospital he helped fund. He once met a man in need in Ethiopia and sponsored his Visa to the U.S. to help him get the medical assistance he needed. He also purchased a run down hotel in a poor U.S. city and turned it into a Retreat/Recovery Camp for the homeless and ex drug offenders. Never wanting to take personal credit, the men and women set free from their addictions due to Mr. Anderson's generosity did not even know of his identity. Upon his death, he was described by loved ones as a "humble and generous man" and a "visionary who trusted the Lord for the results" in the ministries he helped start. The legacy of his generosity is being continued through his children and grandchildren.

Used with the permission of WaterStone. Alias donor name used for anonymity.

Andrea Pauline Kazindra

On a three-month internship in Uganda, University of Colorado Boulder student Andrea Pauline Kazindra discovered

162 orphaned children living in unimaginable conditions. Seeing these children struggle to survive, Andrea knew that something had to change. Instead of waiting for someone else to do something she decided that "being the change" was the answer. She moved to Uganda full time and established Musana Community Development Corporation in 2008. Musana, a national NGO in Uganda and a 501c3 in the US, now employs over 50 Ugandans.

They serve over 500 children and 3,000 community members. Instead of using her degree in Management and International Business from the University of Colorado to chase the American Dream, Andrea is using her passion for social entrepreneurship to fight poverty and bring change in Uganda. Headquartered in Lafayette, Colorado, more info about Musana Community Development Corporation can be found at:

www.musana.org

CHAPTER 5

LEAVING A LEGACY

Sometimes the poorest man leaves his children the richest inheritance.
Ruth E. Renkel

No generation can bequeath to its successor what it has not got.
C.S. Lewis

I want to leave a legacy, How will they remember me?
Did I choose to love? Did I point to You enough,
To make a mark on things?
Nichole Nordeman
Recording artist; lyrics from the song, "Legacy"

A good name is to be chosen rather than great riches, and favor is better than silver or gold.
Proverbs 22:1

Know therefore that the Lord your God is God, the faithful God who keeps covenant and steadfast love with those who love him and keep his commandments, to a thousand generations.
Deuteronomy 7:9

The greatest use of life is to spend it for something that will outlast it.
William James

A Tale of Two Legacies

Jonathan Edwards was born on the 5th day of October, 1703 in the town of East Windsor, Connecticut. Edwards was the fifth of eleven children and the only son of Timothy Edwards and the former Esther Stoddard. His great-great-grandfather,

Richard Edwards, was a pastor in London, whose son William was one of the first men to come to the new colonies in New England in the early 1600's. William had one son, Richard, who became a prosperous merchant. Richard had six daughters and one son named Timothy Edwards, the father of Jonathan Edwards. Timothy graduated from Harvard University in 1661 and pastored a church in East Windsor for sixty-five years. Edwards grandfather on his mother's side was also a pastor, the Reverend Solomon Stoddard of Northampton, Massachusetts.

Edwards grew up in a parsonage on the banks of the Connecticut River where he was educated at home by his parents. He began studying Latin, Greek, and Hebrew at age 6. He also developed a fervent love of nature as his childhood days were filled with exploration of the river, streams, and woods that surrounded his home. At age 12 he entered Yale College where he graduated as the valedictorian and head of his class at age 17.

At age 23, Edwards was ordained as a minister in his grandfather Stoddard's church. As a pastor, Edwards's own church became the largest Protestant church in the world and his spiritual leadership sparked the greatest religious awakening the Western world has ever known. Edwards was married to Sarah Pierrepont when he was 24 and she was 17. Sarah was well known for her beauty, intelligence, character, and commitment to her Christian faith. Evangelist George Whitefield described her as "the most beautiful and noble wife for a Christian minister" that he had ever known. Her children were her life's work as she educated and nurtured them to Christian maturity. It has been said that every great man is supported by a great woman. That was certainly the case for Jonathan Edwards.

Prior to his presidency at Princeton University, Edwards and his family were missionaries in a Native American village for eight years. During their formative years, Jonathan and Sarah educated their children at their home in the village, away from the formal education and social benefits of New England society. In 1758, Edwards died of smallpox at the age of 56. His wife

Sarah died a few weeks later, leaving six of their ten surviving children under age 21 as orphans.

To make matters worse, the oldest Edwards daughter and her husband had both recently died leaving their 2 year old and 4 year old children as orphans. This left the oldest Edwards son, at 20 years of age, responsible for his five younger siblings and his orphaned niece and nephew. Furthermore, Jonathan Edwards died with little money and only left his children with a very modest financial inheritance. According to A.E. Winship, "If Jonathan Edwards did not leave a large financial legacy, he did impart to his children an intellectual capacity and vigor, moral character, and devotion to training which have projected themselves through eight generations without losing the strength and force of their great ancestor. Of the three sons and eight daughters of Jonathan Edwards there was not one, nor a husband or wife of one, whose character and ability, whose purpose and achievement were not a credit to this godly man. Of the seventy-five grandchildren, with their husbands and wives, there was but one for whom an apology may be offered, and nearly everyone was exceptionally strong in scholarship and moral force."

Although the Edwards children faced incredible odds, they faithfully clung to the spiritual legacy and faith in God that had been taught to them by their parents. His three sons all graduated from Princeton and five of his daughters married college graduates. Among Edwards eight sons and sons-in-law, one was president of Princeton, one was president of Union College, four were judges, two were members of the Continental Congress, one was a member of the Massachusetts Revolutionary War Commission, one was a state senator, one was the president of the Connecticut House of Representatives, three were Revolutionary War officers, one was a member of the Constitutional Convention, and one was a pastor.

In future generations, Edward's legacy paid godly dividends as well. According to *A Study in Education and Heredity* by A.E. Winship (1900), the 1,400 descendants of Jonathan Edwards included:

- 300 preachers
- 295 college graduates
- 100 missionaries
- 100 lawyers including 1 law school dean
- 80 public office holders
- 75 military officers
- 65 college professors including 13 college presidents
- 60 prominent authors
- 56 physicians including 1 dean of a medical school
- 30 judges
- 3 U.S. Senators
- 3 governors
- 3 mayors
- 1 comptroller of the U.S. Treasury
- 1 Vice President of the United States

A contrasting legacy can be found in the life of Max Jukes, a man of Dutch origin who lived in New York in the early 1700's. Jukes lived a godless life of crime, hated school, hated to work, loved heavy drinking, did not like preaching, and married an ungodly woman with whom he had five children. Upon the foundation, or lack thereof, of their patriarch Max Jukes, the Jukes family according to Winship, "neglected all religious privileges, defied and antagonized the church and all that it stands for." The Jukes legacy is one of ungodliness, crime, debauchery, ignorance and poverty. In fact, is estimated that the Jukes family cost the state of New York over $1,250,000. The 1,200 descendants of Jukes included:

- 400 men and women physically wrecked by their own wickedness
- 310 paupers and vagrants living in poorhouses for a collective 2,300 years

- 300 infant deaths due to lack of good conditions
- 190 public prostitutes
- 130 convicted criminals
- 100 alcoholics
- 60 habitual thieves who spent an average of 12 years in jail
- 55 victims of impurity
- 7 murderers

Communicate Your Legacy

As an estate administration attorney, I often see unfortunate circumstances where children are fighting tooth and nail over mom and dad's estate. These battles often become nasty and they can affect family relationships for decades. I believe that many, if not most, of these estate disputes could be avoided if mom and dad were willing to communicate their plan to their children during their lifetime. In biblical times, the passing on of assets was a verbal as well as a physical act. The father would verbally communicate his wishes to his children, bless them, and pass his property to them.

The verbal blessing was as important or more important than the transfer of property. In our modern society, most family wealth transfers do not contain any verbal communication or blessing. We simply pass on our assets through legal documents such as Last Wills and Revocable Living Trusts. However, if we really want to leave a legacy, we need to return to these ancient principles and communicate our wishes verbally and in writing. Passing on our values orally and in writing should come in the form of a Family Meeting and Legacy Will, while passing on our property should include creating a legal estate plan that honors God with our possessions.

A recent Wall Street Journal study found that 70% of affluent families' wealth is gone by the end of the second generation and 90% is gone by the end of the third generation. Which means that a failure to effectively communicate your legacy will likely result in devastating losses of both financial and spiritual capital.

Legacy Will™

The contrasting lives of Jonathan Edwards and Max Jukes reminds us that we will all leave a legacy when we leave this world. We are building that legacy every day. The question is, what will your legacy be? Will it simply be a financial inheritance? Or will you leave your children and family with a spiritual inheritance that will make a lasting impact for generations to come?

> *Tell your children of it, and let your children tell their children, and their children to another generation.*
>
> Joel 1:3

Creating a Legacy Will™ is a great way to transfer your values and not just your valuables. A Legacy Will is an expression of your faith and values that you pass on to the next generation.

For thousands of years, the Jewish people engaged in the ancient tradition of passing down their spiritual heritage, values, beliefs, principles, and stories to succeeding generations. The first example of this can be found in Genesis 49 when Jacob blesses his sons while on his deathbed. Originally transmitted orally, this tradition eventually progressed into the written word. Whether oral, written, or some other form of modern media, I tend to think of this tradition as the creation of a Legacy Will.

When we think of planning for our future today, we tend to think about legal documents such as Wills, Trusts, Powers of Attorney, Living Wills, etc. While such documents are essential to a comprehensive estate plan, they are focused on passing on your property but not necessarily your principles. Estate planning is primarily concerned with passing on the "stuff" you accumulate during your lifetime, with little regard for that which is lasting and eternal. A Legacy Will is not a legal document, but it may be more meaningful and fulfilling for your family than any other form of estate planning or life planning that you engage in.

An effective Legacy Will communicates your legacy of faith, ethics, beliefs, life lessons, and spiritual principles. It connects past and future generations through the telling of your unique story. A Legacy Will can take on a variety of forms including: letters, journals, books, stories, videos, audio messages, family bibles, favorite scriptures, scrapbooks, family history book, family tree, or photographs. There is not a specific formula or format when it comes to creating a Legacy Will, however, the following issues may be addressed:

- Articulate your spiritual journey
- Tell your story
- Share important life lessons
- Pass along your values
- Share your most cherished memories
- Ask for and encourage forgiveness
- Advice or direction to future generations
- Share favorite scriptures
- Share favorite books, music, etc.
- Prayers for family members or future generations
- Advice for fulfilling marriages
- Advice for raising children
- Guidance for careers and calling
- Share what God has done in your life
- Expressions of gratitude and love
- Expressions of hope and blessing for future generations
- Communicates your worldview
- Reminds others of your love for them and God's love for them

As you are considering planning your estate, don't neglect to pass along your values with a Legacy Will. Don't put it off for another day. Do it now. If you are young, you can go ahead and get started and add to your Legacy Will over your lifetime. If you are older, now is a good time to reflect on your life and begin preparing this special gift for your loved ones. We all have a story to tell and we will all leave a legacy of some sort. Let your Legacy Will tell your story and remind the next generation of God's faithfulness.

> *One generation shall commend your works to another, and shall declare your mighty acts.*
>
> Psalm 145:4

Life's Time Capsule™

I have found that using a website like Life's Time Capsule™ is a great way to preserve your Legacy Will™ for future generations. Life's Time Capsule allows you to capture your memories, preserve your legacy, and pass along your life. It is a single source repository for organizing, editing & storing your most precious moments. After you upload your photos, videos, voice recordings, and journal entries, you choose how and who you want to share them with. Your information is stored in a secure digital vault and you decide who the recipients will be.

In my opinion, there is a not a better tool to preserve your Legacy Will™. To get started with sharing your legacy through Life's Time Capsule™ visit the following link:
www.LTCapsule.com/legacywill

Family Meeting

Parents are often reluctant to share their estate plans with their adult children. Some may feel it is a private matter, only to be unveiled after their death. Many are afraid of creating relationship problems within the family, for example if one child is chosen to be a trustee or personal representative over the others. But explaining your decisions now to your family, in a general way, will avoid surprises later and make it more likely that they will accept them.

Holding a family meeting is a good way to do this. Ask your estate planning attorney and financial advisor to be there. They will be able to explain how your plan will work and why these decisions were made, as well as answer any questions. This will also introduce your advisors to your family members so they will be more comfortable working together in your absence.

Choose a date and time that is convenient for everyone and a place that is appropriate. The room should encourage discussion but also convey the seriousness of the meeting. Your attorney or financial advisor will probably have access to a meeting room; a family room that accommodates everyone can also work. Limit the meeting to adults; arrange for childcare if necessary. Have a beginning and ending time.

Make a list of topics you want to cover. No specific financial information or values of assets need to be disclosed at this time. This meeting should be a general explanation of what you have planned and why, in order to prepare family members for what they can expect and may need to do if you become disabled or die. Allow for and encourage questions and discussion.

Expect there to be some anxiety as the meeting begins, as these are often sensitive issues. There may be challenges with second marriages and blended families. Or there may be a child that you do not feel is financially ready to handle an inheritance.

If trusts are involved, explain why they are being used. If charitable giving is part of your plan, explain how this is in keeping with your values.

It is important to give your children some idea of the size of any inheritance they may receive. With people living longer and long-term care expenses often lasting for years, there may be little to pass on. If they are expecting a large inheritance, it would be better to give them a realistic picture now rather than later. At the same time, it is helpful to prepare a child if a sizable inheritance is coming their way so they don't go on a spending spree, fall prey to a scam, or become afraid to use the money at all.

Last Words

For each and every one of us, that moment will come, when we say our last words to those that we love. Whether from our own personal experiences or viewed on a movie screen, we know that a person's last words are of great importance. It is the last moment to convey a message that will live beyond the speaker. Last words are transcendent. In many ways, your estate plan is the last word that you leave to your family. Certainly, it is the last written words you leave behind. How will those words be remembered? What is it that you want to show your family with your final directions concerning your earthly things? Will you simply leave behind your property, or will you leave something more lasting and meaningful?

There are many examples in scripture where last words left an eternal legacy for those left behind. Jacob blessed his sons individually just before his death. Prior to his death, Joshua gathered all of the tribes of Israel together and encouraged them to put away foreign gods and pleaded with them to "incline your heart to the Lord, the God of Israel." Joshua then made a covenant with the people that they would follow the Lord after his death. After this had taken place, "Joshua sent the people away, every man to his inheritance." (Joshua 24: 23-33)

Joshua certainly left the people with the Promised Land as a physical inheritance, but the spiritual inheritance, through the covenant to follow the Lord, is what would sustain the nation of Israel for generations to come. This chapter ends with the death and burial of Eleazar, the son of Aaron who was the high priest and brother of Moses. In other words, it is the final chapter of a generation that wandered through the desert hoping for a Promised Land.

Literally and symbolically, one generation is passing the torch to the next. David Guzik puts it this way, "As the generations pass, they are each challenged to conquer the land of blessing and promise that God has for them - and we will do it too, as we pay close heed to our Joshua, to Jesus Christ."

King David's last words to his son Solomon, and the successor to his throne, is another example.

> *When David's time to die drew near, he commanded Solomon his son, saying, "I am about to go the way of all the earth. Be strong, and show yourself a man, and keep the charge of the Lord your God, walking in his ways and keeping his statutes, his commandments, his rules, and his testimonies, as it is written in the Law of Moses, that you may prosper in all that you do and wherever you turn, that the Lord may establish his word that he spoke concerning me, saying, 'If your sons pay close attention to their way, to walk before me in faithfulness with all their heart and with all their soul, you shall not lack a man on the throne of Israel.'*
>
> 1 Kings 2: 1-4

A man after God's own heart, the warrior, the King, calling his son close to his side and reminding him of what is truly important in life; to walk in the ways of the Lord and follow Him with all of his heart and soul. A father passing on a lifelong legacy of faithfully following the Lord even through all of his faults and failings. Endearing his son to be a faithful servant of the true King.

And what about Yeshua? Jesus. The Christ. What about his last words with the fate of the world hanging in the balance? In Matthew 28, before his ascension into heaven, Jesus spoke these words to his disciples:

> *Now the eleven disciples went to Galilee, to the mountain to which Jesus had directed them. And when they saw him they worshiped him, but some doubted. And Jesus came and said to them, "All authority in heaven and on earth has been given to me. Go therefore and make disciples of all nations, baptizing them in the name of the Father and of the Son and of the Holy Spirit, teaching them to observe all that I have commanded you. And behold, I am with you always, to the end of the age."*
>
> Matthew 28: 16-20

Jesus' last words on the earth was the Great Commission to share His gospel to the world. Undoubtedly hanging on His every word, the disciples are told to go and make disciples of all nations. We are called to do likewise with the short time we live on this earth. That is our mission. That is the legacy left to us by our King. And we take great comfort in knowing that in life or death, He is with us to the end of the age.

What about You? What will your last words be? William James said, "The greatest use of life is to spend it for something that will outlast it." What will outlast your life? The answer to that question is the greatest treasure you can leave when you are called home. Most people use their estate plan to pass on stuff, but yours can be used to pass on purpose. It can encourage the next generation to make disciples throughout the earth, until the return of the King.

And now I commend you to God and to the word of his grace, which is able to build you up and to give you the inheritance among all those who are sanctified.

Acts 20:32

Go change the world!

www.LeaveALegacyBook.com

ABOUT THE AUTHOR

Michael L. Smith, Esq. is a licensed Colorado Attorney who provides Estate Planning and Business Planning legal services to clients throughout Colorado. He has helped hundreds of clients form their business or plan their estate.

Mr. Smith holds a B.S. in Business Management from Carson-Newman University, an M.S. in Sport Management from The University of Tennessee, and a J.D. from Liberty University School of Law. Mr. Smith served as the Student Bar Association President while attending Liberty University School of Law.

Additionally, in 2006, Mr. Smith served in the White House as an intern in the Presidential Personnel Office. While at the White House, Mr. Smith assisted in recruiting executives to serve the President in the U.S. Department of Commerce, the U.S. Department of the Treasury, and the U.S. Department of Transportation.

Michael is the founder of Veritas Law Group, LLC in Colorado Springs, CO (www.VeritasLawColorado.com). The firm represents estate planning and business clients throughout Colorado. Michael frequently speaks to church and other community groups about the integration of estate planning and Christian generosity.

Michael lives in Colorado Springs with his wife and four boys. In his free time, he can be found coaching his kid's sports teams, fly-fishing, snowboarding, hiking, and camping with his family in the Rocky Mountains.

MichaelLSmithEsq@gmail.com

ABOUT VERITAS LAW GROUP, LLC

Veritas is the Latin word for truth, particularly of a transcendent character. It embodies the ideals of honesty, integrity and precision. Those ideals form the foundation for Veritas Law Group. At Veritas Law Group our goal is to provide each of our clients with wise counsel and customized legal solutions. Whether you are building your business or planning your estate, we are here to help you live a legacy so that you can leave a legacy.

www.VeritasLawColorado.com

Appendix A

Estate Planning Terms

Attorney-in-Fact - An individual designated in a power of attorney to act as the agent of the person who executed the document.

Basic Will - A will that distributes everything to your spouse, if living, otherwise to your children when they reach the age of majority.

Beneficiary - A person who receives funds, property, or other benefits from a will, trust, contract, or insurance policy.

Bond - A special insurance policy that insures against the Executor stealing or losing money from the estate.

Codicil - An amendment to a will.

Contingent Beneficiary - A beneficiary of estate property who only has the right to receive estate property upon the occurrence of an event.

Decedent - A person who has died.

Durable Power of Attorney for Health Care - A written document in which an individual designates another person to make health care and health-related decisions in the event that the individual becomes incapacitated.

Durable Power of Attorney for Property (Financial) - A written document in which an individual designates another person to make his or her financial/property and property-related decisions in the event that the individual becomes incapacitated and is unable to do so.

Estate - An individual's property and assets including real estate, bank accounts, life insurance policies, stocks, retirement accounts, and personal property such as automobiles and jewelry.

Estate Tax – A federal tax that is imposed at a person's death based upon their assets left behind.

Executor - A person named in a will who is authorized to manage the estate of the deceased person. The executor will collect the property, pay off any debts, and distribute property and assets according to the terms of the will. (aka "Personal Representative")

Fee Simple - The entire or whole ownership of property unburdened by any future interest or any possibility of losing total ownership. This is the highest form of property ownership. Other forms of property ownership are life estate, leasehold interest, or tenancy in common, for example.

Fiduciary - A person or institution that is legally responsible for the management, investment, and distribution of funds primarily for the benefit of another (i.e. the trustee identified in a trust).

Grantor - A person who transfers assets to another, usually into a trust. Also may be called a trustor or settlor.

Guardian - An individual with the legal authority and responsibility to care for another, usually a minor child.

Heir - A person who would inherit property under state intestacy law, where a person dies without a will.

Incapacity - A person's inability to act on his or her own behalf. A court makes a finding of incapacity.

Intestate - A term used when a person dies without a will.

Issue - All descendents of a particular person. The term includes children, grandchildren, and other descendants.

Joint Tenancy With Right of Survivorship - A title that is often placed on co-owned property. At the death of one owner, the other owner will be legally entitled to sole possession of the property, regardless of what provisions are made in a will. A husband and wife often use this form of ownership.

Memorandum of Disposition - A separate writing or memorandum which disposes of tangible personal property upon a person's death. It is not legally binding, however, the executor is instructed to distribute tangible personal property according to the memorandum if one is in existence.

Outside of the Will - Some property passes outside of the specifications in a will. The beneficiary of such property is determined by your directions (beneficiary designations) when you opened the financial account (or acquired the property) and not by your Last Will & Testament. This may include P.O.D. accounts (see below), certificates of deposit, bank accounts, retirement accounts, annuity contracts, life insurance, and property held as joint tenants with right of survivorship. Beneficiary designations should be updated on all such assets to reflect the wishes of the owner.

Payable on Death (P.O.D.) - Many financial accounts are "P.O.D." accounts. This means that the account will go to the person you designate as the beneficiary on the account records with the bank, broker, or insurance agent, and not in accordance with your will. Also called Transfer on Death or "T.O.D." accounts.

Per Capita - Per capita is another Latin term that means "by the head". The living members in a class of beneficiaries who are closest in relationship to the testator (typically children) will receive an equal share. However, if a member in this class of beneficiaries predeceases the testator, such member's share will be used to increase the remaining member's shares in this same class. The deceased member's share will not pass by representation to their heirs (children). In other words, in a typical family situation the children of the deceased parent (who would also be the grandchildren of the testator) would be disinherited.

Per Capita at Each Generation- A newer system of distribution known as per capita at each generation has been adopted by a few states, including Colorado, and the Uniform Probate Code. This approach views the family horizontally and treats equally those who are equally distant from the testator. The initial division of shares is made at the level where one or more descendants are alive. However, the shares of deceased beneficiaries at that same level are treated as one pot and are dropped down and divided equally among the representatives on the next generational level.

Per Stirpes - Per Stirpes is a Latin term that technically means "by the roots or by representation". This approach views the family vertically. The living members in a class of beneficiaries who are closest in relationship to the testator (typically children) will receive an equal share. However, if a member in the class of beneficiaries who are closest in relationship to the testator predeceases the testator, such members issue (children; who would also be grandchildren of the testator) take by representation what their deceased parent would have taken.

Personal Representative - A person, who, after your death, collects all your assets, pays all your bills and distributes the balance as you direct in your will.

Power of Attorney - A written document that gives one person the legal authority to act on behalf of another person.

Probate - A process whereby a court reviews a will to make sure that it is authentic, allows others to make legal challenges to the will, and ensures that the instructions in the will are properly carried out by the executor.

Self Proving Affidavit - An attachment to a Last Will & Testament that eliminates the need for the witnesses to a will to be found and sign a formal document answering several questions when the will is offered for probate.

Testator - Someone who makes or has made a Will, or one who dies leaving a Will.

Trust - A written document providing that property be held by one (the "trustee") for the benefit of another (the "beneficiary"). A trust may be created during the grantor's lifetime or after his or her death.

Trustee - A person named in a trust document who will manage property owned by the trust, and distribute the trust income or property according to the terms of the trust document. A trustee may be an individual or a business.

Will - A document that directs how property shall be distributed upon a deceased person's death.

Appendix B

Intestate Succession in Colorado
C.R.S. §15-11-102 and 103

If you die with:	This is who inherits your estate:
A spouse but no descendants (i.e. children or grandchildren) or parents	Spouse inherits everything
A spouse and descendants from you and that spouse, and the spouse has no other descendants	Spouse inherits everything
A spouse and one or both parents	Spouse inherits the first $300,000 of your intestate property plus ¾ of the balance. Your parents inherit the remainder.
A spouse and descendants from you and that spouse, and the spouse has descendants from another relationship	Spouse inherits the first $225,000 of your intestate property plus ½ of the balance. Your descendants inherit the remainder.
A spouse and descendant(s) from you and someone other than that spouse (i.e., a child from another relationship)	Spouse inherits the first $150,000 of your intestate property plus ½ of the balance. Your descendants inherit the remainder.
Children but no spouse	Children inherit everything. If a child predeceased you, their children (i.e., your grandchildren) receive their deceased parent's share.
Parents but no spouse or descendants	Parents inherit everything
Siblings but no spouse, descendants, or parents	Siblings inherit everything

Appendix C

Credit Shelter Trust Estate Flow Chart

Estate of Husband & Wife/**When Husband Dies:**

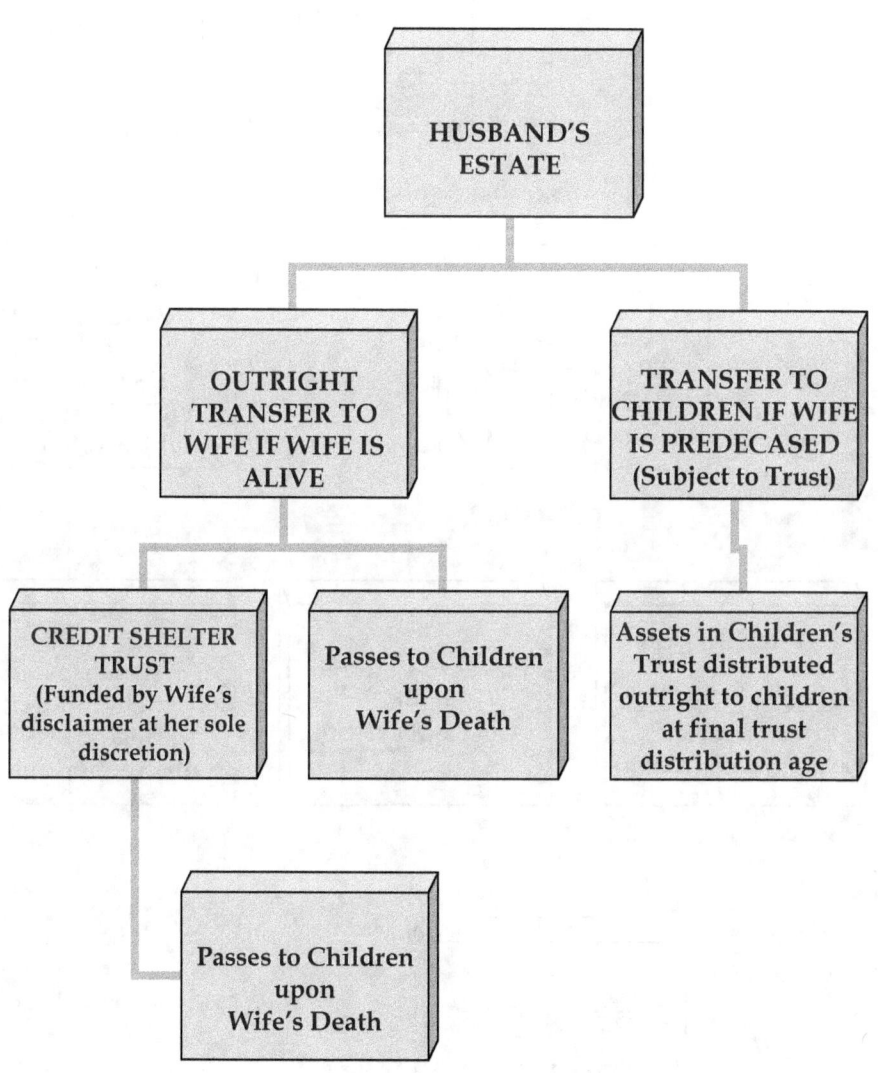

Appendix C continued

Estate of Husband & Wife/**When Wife Dies:**

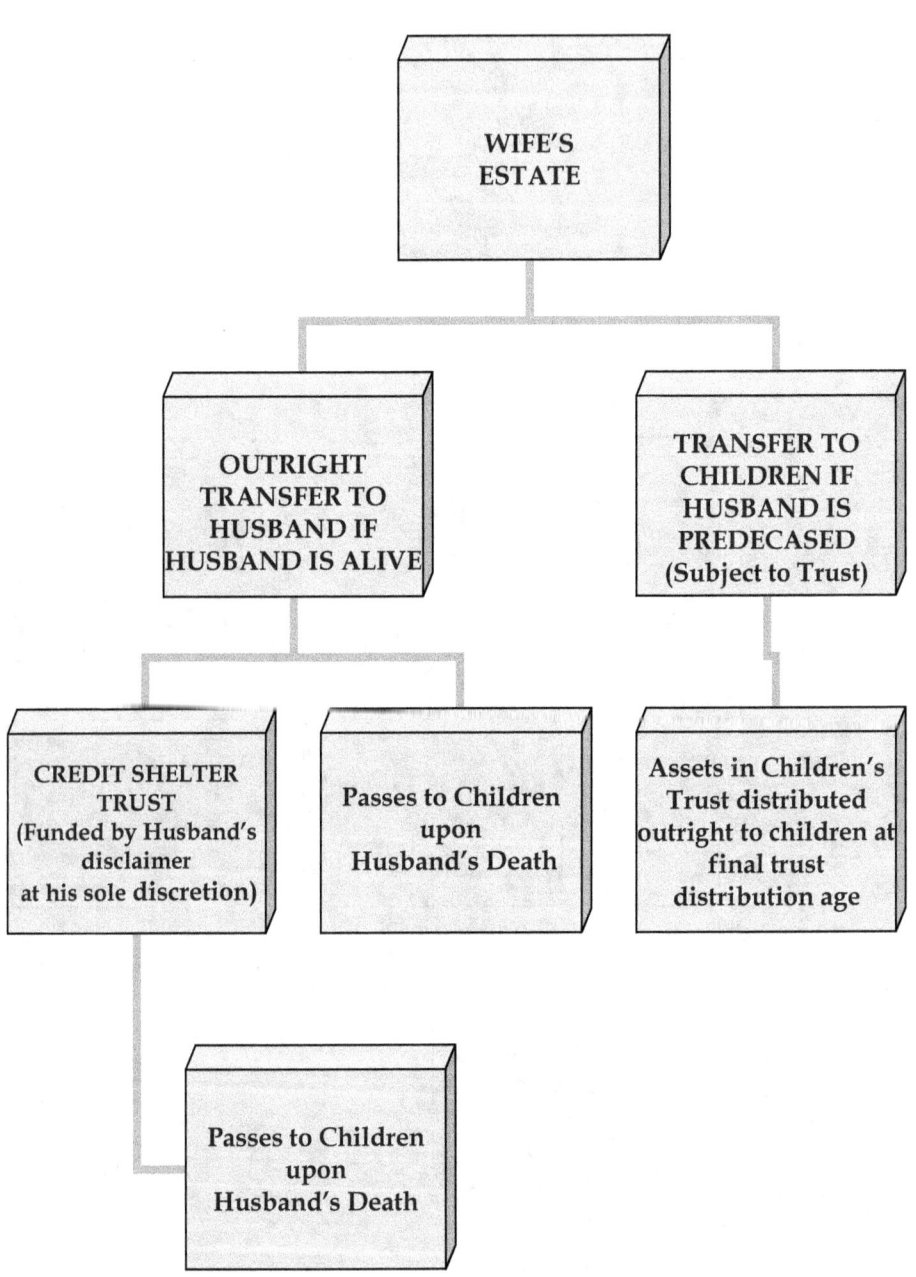

Appendix D

Charitable Remainder Trust
With Wealth Replacement Life Insurance Trust

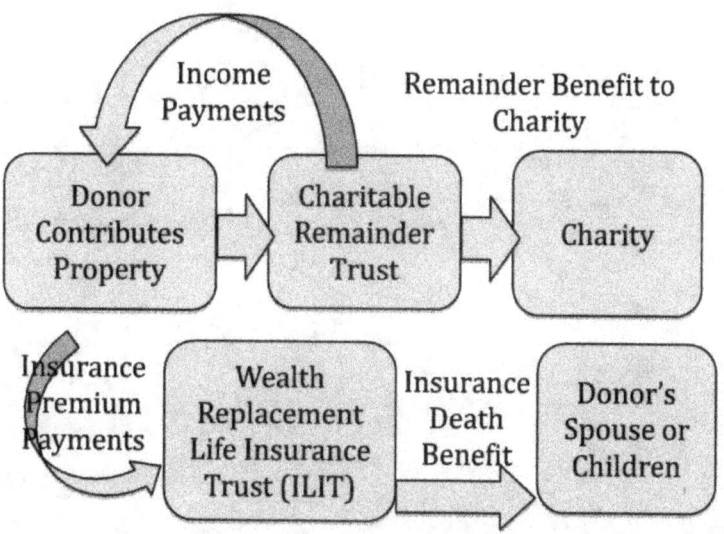

Appendix E

Charitable Lead Trust

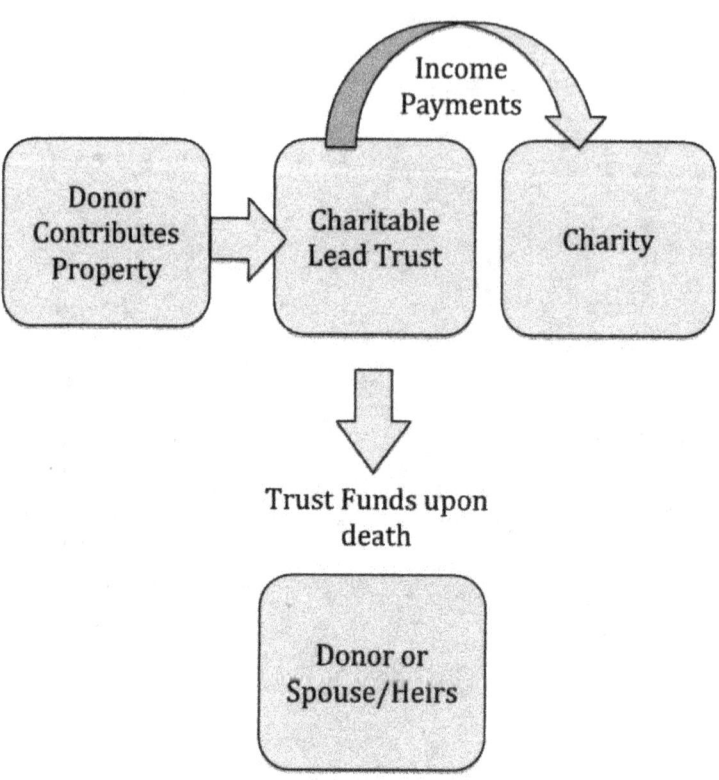

Appendix F

Federal Estate Tax Chart 2013-2016

	2013	2014	2015	2016
Estate Tax Exemption *	$5.25M	$5.34M	$5.43M	$5.66M
Maximum Estate Tax Rate	40%	40%	40%	40%
Lifetime Gift Tax Exemption	$5.25M	$5.34M	$5.43M	$5.66M
Maximum Gift Tax Rate	40%	40%	40%	40%
Annual Gift Tax Exclusion Amount **	$14,000 or $28,000 per married couple	$14,000 or $28,000 per married couple	$14,000 or $28,000 per married couple	$14,000 or $28,000 per married couple
Generation Skipping Tax Exemption	$5.25M	$5.34M	$5.43M	$5.66M
Maximum GST Rate	40%	40%	40%	40%

* Amounts are estimates indexed for inflation.

** Annual Gift Tax Exclusion amounts subject to increase with inflation.

Appendix G

Colorado Spousal Elective Share
C.R.S. §15-11-201

Number of Years Married	Elective Share %
Less than 1 year	Supplemental Amount*
1 year but less than 2 years	5% of augmented estate
2 years but less than 3 years	10% of augmented estate
3 years but less than 4 years	15% of augmented estate
4 years but less than 5 years	20% of augmented estate
5 years but less than 6 years	25% of augmented estate
6 years but less than 7 years	30% of augmented estate
7 years but less than 8 years	35% of augmented estate
8 years but less than 9 years	40% of augmented estate
9 years but less than 10 years	45% of augmented estate
10 years or more	50% of augmented estate

* To offset the possibly harsh results of the vesting schedule for short-term marriages, the elective-share statutes provide a "supplemental elective-share amount" which gives the spouse a minimum of $52,000 (subject to a reduction by property otherwise passing to or owned by the spouse). Other states have very similar statutes which serve to protect the surviving spouse.

Appendix H

Donor-Advised Funds vs. Private Foundations

	Donor-Advised Funds	**Private Foundations**
Start-Up Time	Immediate	Weeks or Several months due to IRS required paperwork
Start-Up Costs	Nothing	Legal fees can become substantial
Tax Deduction Limits for Gifts of Cash	50% of adjusted gross income	30% of adjusted gross income
Tax Deduction Limits For Gifts of Stock or Real Property	30% of adjusted gross income	20% of adjusted gross income
Valuation of Gifts	Fair Market Value	Fair Market Value for publicly traded stocks, donor's cost basis for all other gifts
Required Grant Distribution	None	5% of net asset value annually, regardless of what the assets earn
Privacy	Can be confidential and anonymous	Must file IRS Form 990-PF; public record
Administrative Responsibility for Donor	Recommend grants to Christian Charitable causes as the Spirit leads	Manage assets, keep detailed records, file tax returns, maintain corporate formalities
Excise Tax	None	1% to 2% of investment income annually
Control of Grants and Assets	Donor recommends grants, but the sponsoring charity has the final authority	Donor and family have complete control over grants and investments

Appendix I

Federal Income Tax Deductions for Charitable Gifts

	PUBLIC CHARITIES (Donor Advised Funds)	PRIVATE FOUNDATIONS
Type of Property Contributed to Charitable Trust	Percentage of the Contribution that is income tax deductible	Percentage of the Contribution that is income tax deductible
Cash	50% of Adjusted Gross Income*	30% of Adjusted Gross Income*
Appreciated Property (i.e., Long-Term Capital Gain Property)**	30% of Adjusted Gross Income*	20% of Adjusted Gross Income*
Real Property donated under Conservation Easement	50% of Adjusted Gross Income for individuals and 100% for farmers and ranchers***	N/A

* The income tax deduction can be carried forward in future tax years for up to 5 years.
** Property that has been held for at least one year that would have yielded a long-term capital gains tax if sold. This could include real estate, stocks, bonds, etc.
***The income tax deduction can be carried forward for 15 years. Qualified ranchers and farmers are defined as someone who receives more than 50% of their income from the "trade or business of farming".

SOURCES

https://www.barna.org/barna-update/congregations/41-new-study-shows-trends-in-tithing-and-donating#.VGJlQjnND8E

http://abcnews.go.com/Health/arizona-accident-victim-emerges-coma-poised-donate-organs/story?id=15208351

http://www.today.com/id/20689992/ns/today-today_news/t/doctors-pull-plug-comatose-woman-wakes/#.VGJktjnND8E

http://www.jdgreear.com/my_weblog/2011/09/the-generosity-matrix.html

http://infomotions.com/etexts/gutenberg/dirs/1/5/6/2/15623/15623.htm

www.ingramcontent.com/pod-product-compliance
Lightning Source LLC
Chambersburg PA
CBHW071758200526
45167CB00017B/432